Petitioning For Our Rights, Fighting For Our Nation:
The History of the Democratic Union of Cameroonian Women, 1949-1960

Meredith Terretta

Langaa Research & Publishing CIG
Mankon, Bamenda

Publisher
Langaa RPCIG
Langaa Research & Publishing Common Initiative Group
P.O. Box 902 Mankon
Bamenda
North West Region
Cameroon
Langaagrp@gmail.com
www.langaa-rpcig.net

Distributed in and outside N. America by African Books Collective
orders@africanbookscollective.com
www.africanbookcollective.com

ISBN:9956-728-05-5

DISCLAIMER
All views expressed in this publication are those of the author and do
not necessarily reflect the views of Langaa RPCIG.

Table of Contents

Preface

The absence of women in the history of Cameroon has been a cause for concern for Cameroonian women and feminists. There have been speculations about their involvement in anti-colonial struggles in the 1950s especially in scheming with or hiding men or in transporting arms, but existing historical studies have not foregrounded the role of women. Cameroon and African feminists have been thirsty for concrete information to prove the active participation of women in the struggle for independence.

This book comes as a thirst quencher by showing that, far from occupying marginal positions, Cameroonian women played a central role in the history of Cameroonian and African politics. Meredith Terretta has shown, in her analysis of the Democratic Union of Cameroonian Women (UDEFEC) that Cameroonian women, although largely illiterate, PETITIONED FOR OUR RIGHTS AND FOUGHT FOR OUR NATION. THEY served as intermediaries between the burgeoning collective imagination of emancipation from foreign rule and the practical realization of that emancipation. The UDEFEC women - working at home, in the markets, in the fields, in city shops, colonialists' households, or schools – actively helped to reshape social ideology until the nationalist message became something "thinkable" even in the humblest village home. They contributed to the fight for independence through petitions written to the United Nations, through their organization of street protests, through their participation in political meetings. Cameroonian women contributed to socio-economic as well as political change in independence era Cameroon.

Dr Atanga, Lem Lilian,
Senior Lecturer, Gender and Discourse Studies
Department of African Studies,
University of Dschang, Cameroon

Acknowledgments

Funding from the Global Studies Program at the University of Wisconsin-Madison enabled me to conduct preliminary research in 1999 upon which this work is based. The Jacob K. Javits Fellowship and the University Fellowship from the Graduate School and the Department of History at the University of Wisconsin-Madison also provided support for the research, course work, and writing of this work.

In Cameroon, I thank the many who supported me in putting together this work: Winsome Bammel, Marceline Betene, Monita and Perry Burtch, Emmanuel Chia, Odile Chatap-Ekindi, Camille Ekindi, Henriette Ekwe, his majesty the late *Fo* Feze of Bandenkop, Basile Louka, Gérard and Rebecca Mbarga, Marie-Irène Ngapeth-Biyong, Kathleen Ngu-Blanchett, Mafo Claude Njiké-Bergeret, the Ondos, Dieudonné Pouhe Pouhe, Maurice Takam, Nicaise Ngayo Teclaire, Jean-Bosco Tchientchieu of the *Archives Nationales de Yaoundé*, Jules Wache, and his majesty the late *Fo* Tchatchouang Waton of Bangwa. In France, I am grateful to Marc Michel and Chantal Ndami. In Madison, I thank Edward Duesterhoeft who aided me in negotiating the micro-print series, Professor Stanlie James who brought the Memorial Union Library's collection to my attention, and Beth Harper who helped me find my way around the unwieldy UN indexes. For all kinds of aid and encouragement at various times during this project, academic, editorial and otherwise I have benefited from the advice and friendship of Florence Bernault, Bolaji Campbell, Martin Daly, Rachel Demotts, Pamela Feldman-Savelsberg, Becky and Larry Ingle, Stanlie James, Ousman Kobo, Dior Konate, Emilie Ngo-

Nguidjol, Mukoma wa Ngugi, Peter Quella, Ryan Ronnenberg, Penelope Pack, Michael Schatzberg, Aliko Songolo, Cheryl Sterling, Stephen Volz, Peter Quella, and Tresor Yoassi.

Abbreviations

ALNK Armée de Libération Nationale du Kamerun
CGT Confédération Générale du Travail
CNO Comité National d'Organisation
ESOCAM Evolution sociale camerounaise
JDC Jeunesse démocratique camerounaise
JEUCAFRA Jeunesse camerounaise française
MDC Mouvement démocratique camerounais
MRP Mouvement républicain populaire
PCF Parti communiste français
RDA Rassemblement démocratique africain
UDEFEC Union démocratique des Femmes camerounaises
UDHR Universal Declaration of Human Rights
UNGA United Nations General Assembly
UNICAFRA Union camerounaise française
UNTC United Nations Trusteeship Council
UPC Union des Populations du Cameroun
USCC Union des Syndicats Confédérés du Cameroun

x

Chapter 1

Introduction
Cameroonian Women and the Writing of a
Popular Nationalism

After the United Nations (UN) Charter of 1946 established the British Cameroons and French Cameroon as trusteeship territories under the international supervision of the UN, Cameroonians began to address the UN Trusteeship Council by way of petitions. These petitions originated from individuals and groups in diverse regions throughout the country, and reflected the ambivalent attitudes of the petitioners towards their European administrators. The Trusteeship years ushered a new political consciousness into the Cameroons, manifested by the formation of political parties, social organizations, and labor unions following the Second World War. The conservative *Evolution social camerounaise* (ESOCAM) and the anti-colonial, nationalist *Union des populations du Cameroun (*UPC) represented the two extremes of political thinking during this formative era. ESOCAM, comprised of a handful of elite evolués, [1]

---

[1] French assimilationist colonial policy designated as *évolués* those Africans who qualified as "literate elites" who lived under the jurisdiction of French civil code. The Ministry of the Colonies' purpose was to promote the assimilation of "civilized" European values, and thereby ensure colonial elite's permanent loyalty to France. The remaining majority of the population were "subjects," and were therefore subject to greater disciplinary measures and a stricter penal code than the *évolués*, including, after 1924, the forced donation of labor to the administration, known as the *indigénat*. See Edward Mortimer, *France and the Africans 1944-1960: A Political History*, London, 1969, 37-40; Hubert Deschamps, "French Colonial Policy in Tropical Africa Between the Two World Wars," in

1

supported the French administration in cautious preparation for eventual autonomy in a civilization that would closely resemble France's.

On the opposite end of the political spectrum, Ruben Um Nyobé's UPC organized as a popular movement, with several collaborating wings, including the *Union démocratique des femmes camerounaises* (UDEFEC), the *Jeunesse democratique camerounaise* (JDC), and the *Union des Syndicats Confédérés du Cameroun* (USCC). From its inception, UPC leaders and members understood that Trusteeship status differentiated the Cameroon territories from other British and French colonies in Africa. UPC activists promoted an awareness of this international status along with its nationalist and anti-colonialist message, creating a multi-layered ideology that spread throughout the territory during the 1950s. Ruben Um Nyobé and other leaders of the UPC familiarized themselves with the UN Charter, focusing on Article 76 that promised eventual autonomy to the Trusteeship territories. The UPC demanded independence for the Cameroonian territories, with a target date of 1956, and the reunification of the British and French territories.

Ruben Um Nyobé served as the fountainhead of the movement from its inception, and his ideas for political and economic emancipation of French Cameroon guided the movement until his death in 1958. Born in the Sanaga-Maritime around 1913, Ruben Um Nyobé attended

---

Prosser Gifford and William Roger Louis, eds., *France and Britain in Africa: Imperial Rivalry and Colonial Rule,* New Haven and London, 1971. For an analysis of this policy and an enlightening contrast with British administrative policy in Cameroon, particularly as it affected literacy rates in the two territories, see Richard Bjornson, *The African Quest for Freedom and Identity: Cameroonian Writing and the National Experience,* Bloomington, 1991, chap. 2.

Presbyterian schools in the area, but was primarily self-educated. By the 1930s he had acquired a position as a low level civil servant, and eventually served as a court clerk in Yaounde and Edea. [2] The UPC and its affiliates were organized in a pyramid structure, from local committees in small villages or urban neighborhoods, to larger regional committees, with a directors' committee at the top. Committee leaders were elected by members' votes at meetings, and traveling delegations updated local meetings on the activities of UPC, UDEFEC, and JDC members beyond their region. The movement gained in grassroots level popularity throughout the 1950s, as local committees formed across the territories. The popularity of the party was linked to Um Nyobé's charismatic leadership. In the Sanaga-Maritime rumors circulated about his supernatural powers, and beyond, his popularity increased as he traveled to New York in 1952 and 1953 to speak on behalf of the Cameroonian people before the UN General Assembly, the Fourth Committee devoted to colonial questions, and the Trusteeship Council. Upon his return from trips abroad, he organized UPC congressional meetings throughout the territory to give public accounts of his hearings at the UN.

From its origins, the nationalist party met with opposition from the French administration. Members found themselves discriminated against when applying for business licenses, and believed the local and territorial elections in 1951 and 1952 to have been rigged against their candidates. [3] This repression awakened nationalists' increasingly militant protests against

---

[2] For a thorough biographical sketch of Ruben Um Nyobé see Achille Mbembe, "Introduction," in Ruben Um Nyobé, *Le Problème National Kamerunais,* Paris, 1984, 18-25.

[3] Richard A. Joseph, *Radical Nationalism in Cameroun: Social Origins of the UPC Rebellion,* Oxford: Clarendon Press, 1977.

foreign administrators, which in turn intensified the oppressive strategies of French administrators. Threatened by the movement's rapid growth, the French administration banned the UPC, UDEFEC, the JDC, and the USCC by decree on 13 July 1955 and unleashed violent persecution, by harassment, arrest, imprisonment, and execution, on the nationalists. Many of the movement's leaders escaped into the British Cameroons where they formed a directors' committee in exile at Kumba. Ruben Um Nyobé went into hiding in Babimbi, the Sanaga-Maritime, region of his birth.[4]

From the *maquis*, as nationalists called the underground resistance, Um Nyobé continued to advise the movement with his writings, and remained in communication with the directors' committee at Kumba. In June 1957, the British administration banned the movement in the British Cameroons, and forced the leaders into exile in Sudan. In 1958, the French launched a strategy of systematic "pacification" of the Sanaga-Maritime, forcing most of the population to relocate from their villages and resettle along the roads under French surveillance. The French administration and military troops under its direction collaborated with local informants to locate and assassinate Ruben Um Nyobé on 13 September 1958. Despite the disappearance of the movement's leaders, members

---

[4] Babimbi refers to a subdivision within the region of the Sanaga-Maritime. In this work, the "Bassa region," never an official administrative designation, will refer to the general area of the Sanaga-Maritime and Nyong-et-Kelle. See Achille Mbembe, "Pouvoir des morts et langage des vivants: Les errances de la mémoire nationaliste au Cameroun," in Jean-François Bayart, et al. eds., *Le politique par le bas: Contributions a une problématique de la démocratie*, Paris, 1992, 183-229, for a clear description of this region and its inhabitants.

continued the struggle for independence, using both words and weapons.

The party relied on two innovative strategies to distribute and popularize its message throughout Cameroon: the assignment of key roles to women and youth in the struggle for independence, and the composition and circulation of petitions to the UN from party members. The articulation of these two strategies can be understood through an analysis of UDEFEC, the women's wing of the party. As the women's wing increased in size and strength, so did the number of petitions sent to the UN from UDEFEC members. Reciprocally, UDEFEC party leaders relied on the act of petitioning to increase the vitality, credibility and popularity of the party. Both the active role of women, and the importance of petitioning illustrate the distribution of the UPC message and ideology radiating from city to village, from region to region, permeating class divides as it did gender divides and regionalism. Through UDEFEC, Cameroonian women nationalists played an active role in pre-independence politics, and brought women's specific concerns to the forefront of the struggle against colonialism.

This book historicizes UDEFEC's vital role in the UPC's independence movement. Relying primarily on the petitions women nationalists sent to the UN during the 1950s, it shows how UDEFEC women's political and social activism contributed to a reshaping of the collective consciousness. UDEFEC's role has been overlooked by most of the historical and political analyses of Cameroon during the period leading up to independence.[5] Richard Joseph's political

---

[5] See Susan Geiger, "Women and African Nationalism," *Journal of Women's History* 2.1 (1990): 227-244, for a review of the historiography, up to 1990, of African women in politics. Geiger reveals the shortcomings of the

analysis of the UPC published in 1977, for example, refers briefly to UDEFEC as the female companion to the UPC that served to gain a more uniform base of popular support. But Joseph does not explain the importance of women's participation in popularizing the movement.[6] Nor does he explore the ways in which UDEFEC went beyond the UPC's political platform to speak specifically for Cameroonian women. Jean-François Bayart's seminal analysis of the formation of the Cameroonian state under the first president, Ahmadou Ahidjo, only discusses women within the larger category of *cadets sociaux* as members of social groups that had little access to power and prestige.[7] However, Bayart focuses on the post-colonial era, and does not explain the limited role played by women in the state, a phenomenon that is all the more strange when contrasted with their large scale participation in pre-independence politics. Achille Mbembe provides a historical analysis of movement's cultural characteristics in the Sanaga-Maritime, Um Nyobé's birthplace and the movement's stronghold. Although he first learned UPC history through the songs his grandmother sang during his childhood, Mbembe all but excludes women from his study.[8]

Evaluating the role of women in the Cameroonian nationalist movement reinforces Mbembe's emphasis on the imaginary as a way to historicize the UPC's grassroots

---

literature to explain the spread of nationalism due to the lack of focus on African women's role in politics and nationalist movements. See also Geiger, *TANU Women: Gender and Culture in the Making of Tanganyikan Nationalism, 1955-1965*, Portsmouth, NH, 1997.

[6] Joseph, *Radical Nationalism.*

[7] Jean-François Bayart, *L'Etat au Cameroun* [1979], Paris, 1985.

[8] Achille Mbembe, *La naissance du maquis dans le Sud-Cameroun. 1920-1960*, Paris, 1996 and Achille Mbembe, "Introduction" in *Ecrits sous maquis*, by Ruben Um Nyobé, Paris: L'Harmattan, 1989, 16.

struggle to create an anti-colonial Cameroonian collective consciousness.[9] For Mbembe, African revolution took place within the minds of its participants, and consisted of a radical reshaping of thinking. For Mbembe, the African opposition to colonialism can only be understood in the "imaginary" order, that is by reading symbols, narratives, modes of expression, and behaviors of African actors to piece together the evolution of an ideology that not only rejects colonialism, but creates a separate ideological terrain for discourse and interaction. This thought revolution occurred first and foremost in the imagination of colonial subjects – that area beyond the reach of the colonial system of dominance.[10] Mbembe associates this imaginary order with cultural resources that reference African traditions, particularly those within the invisible sphere of the supernatural, night, and "doubling."[11] As the fight against colonial dominance progressed, Cameroonians drew upon this cultural reservoir of the "traditional," the invisible, and the imaginary to

---

[9] See Achille Mbembe, "Pouvoir." Mbembe describes a nationalist agenda that organized its interests around "the Cameroonian nation perceived as a mythical entity to be realized or a project to achieve an existence free from any sort of foreign administration [my translation]," an event that marked a divergence between the symbolic order of colonialism as opposed to the anti-colonial "imaginary" that envisioned independence.

[10] For more on the political imaginary, see Mbembe, *Naissance*, chaps. 11 and 12; Mbembe. "Domaines de la nuit et autorité onirique dans les maquis du Sud-Cameroun (1955-1958)," *Journal of African History* 31.1 (1991): 89-121; and Mbembe, *De la postcolonie: Essai sur l'imagination politique dans l'Afrique contemporaine,* Paris, 2000. See also chaps. 3 and 5, below.

[11] These are references to the idea of a person having an invisible "double" that resolves conflicts or avenges wrongs during the night, a widespread belief for healers, "witches" and sorcerers in southern Cameroon. See Mbembe, *Naissance*, 384; Eric de Rosny, *L'Afrique des guérisons*, Paris, 1992; and Peter Geschiere, *The Modernity of Witchcraft: Politics and the Occult in Postcolonial Africa*, Charlottesville, 1997.

demonstrate aspects of the social structure that remained free of colonialism's effects.[12]

Cameroonian women served as intermediaries between the burgeoning collective imagination of emancipation from foreign rule and the practical realization of that emancipation. UDEFEC women - working at home, in the markets, in the fields, in city shops, in colonialists' households, or in schools - occupied strategic positions in reshaping social ideology until the UPC message became something "thinkable" even in the humblest village home.[13] No grievance or locale was too small or removed from the realm of Cameroonian politics to be addressed by the party, and herein lay the strength of Um Nyobé's vision. The re-appropriation of Cameroonian ideology took place, not only in the urban centers of Douala, Yaoundé and Kumba, but within the household, as women expressed their distrust of European medicine, protested against restrictions placed on women's commerce and cultivation, and advocated for the future of their children.

Women's roles became all the more crucial as the French and British administrations arrested and executed more and more male leaders of the UPC. Those women fortunate enough to avoid arrest themselves carried on the struggle, and vehemently appealed to the UN for the release of their husbands whom they understood to be unjustly imprisoned, tortured, forced into exile, or even executed for their political beliefs. In the absence of their husbands, these women at

---

[12] See Mbembe, *Naissance*, 362, 401-402: "More than the rites themselves, it was the imaginary that underlay them that was reactivated [my translation]."

[13] Schatzberg posits a "moral matrix" defining what is politically "thinkable" or "unthinkable" for a given society at a given time. See Michael G. Schatzberg, *Political Legitimacy in Middle Africa: Father, Family, Food*, Bloomington, 2001, chap. 1.

once assumed roles as leaders of households and of the nationalist movement. Protectors of biological and agricultural fertility, UDEFEC women emphasized their roles as mothers, wives, or widows, particularly when these roles were affected by European repression of the movement through the administrations' perceived attack on fertility, or when wives lost their husbands to imprisonment or death. The explosion of petitions to the UN over the years demonstrated the expansion of the nationalist movement's popularity. The act of petitioning itself promoted the evolution of Cameroonian political consciousness guided by the UPC and the women of UDEFEC. The petitions built a bridge between Cameroonian nationalism at its grassroots, and the international discussion of human rights and the right to self-determination for colonized peoples.

The Act of Petitioning: A Harbinger of Social and Political Change

In most places and eras throughout the world's history, the act of petitioning has usually represented popular participation in politics, from various groups and individuals pleading their case before a particular authority. U.S. legal historian Gregory Mark evaluates the historical significance of petitions in the making of the American constitutional government: "Understood properly, [the history of the act of petitioning] tells us about popular participation in politics, especially by disenfranchised groups such as women and African Americans, that has remained invisible because of our contemporary fixation on voting as the measure of political participation." [14] Other historians have evaluated petitioning as an act that served the population in times of crisis, political transformation, or during the advent of a new moral economy. [15] These authors and others focus on petitioning as an act that includes the assembly of the signers, implies the spread of a political idea, and brings about a sense of inclusion in a common purpose. To be effective, a petition has to mention the ruler or ruling body it is addressed to, the request, perhaps a motivation and certainly the name (and often other qualities) of the petitioners. These data make petitions a valuable historical source.

Certainly, the petitions from Cameroonians contained aspects of these principles. However, the petitions were addressed, not to a ruler or ruling body, the French or British administrations, but rather to a third party outside the territory, the UN Trusteeship Council. That Cameroonians addressed their petitions to an international party outside their territory prompted them to conceive of the French and British Administering Authorities as outsiders within their territory, and non-essential to Cameroonian political process.

Moreover, from the first tentative petitions sent - 16 were processed by the Trusteeship Council in 1951 - the number

---

[14] Gregory Mark, "The Vestigial Constitution: The History and Significance of the Right to Petition," *Fordham Law Review* 66 (1998): 2153-2230.

[15] See, for post-revolutionary France, Suzanne Desan, "Reconstituting the Social after the Terror: Family, Property and the Law in Popular Politics," *Past and Present: A Journal of Historical Studies* 164, Aug 1999: 81-121; Ruth Bogin, "Petitioning and the New Moral Economy of Post-Revolutionary America," *The William and Mary Quarterly* 45.3 (1998): 391-425; Betty Wood, "White Women, Black Slaves, and the Law in Early National Georgia: The Sunbury Petition of 1791," *The Historical Journal* 35.3 (1992): 611-22.

increased exponentially to over 45,000 in the year of 1956, [16] prompting the Committee to adopt a new procedure of sorting and responding to the petitions topically, rather than individually.[17] The vast majority of these petitions came from the UPC, the JDC, and UDEFEC, and demanded independence and reunification of the British and French territories of the Cameroons. When the parties were banned by the French administration on 13 July 1955, they faced severe punishment for continuing to petition the UN. The leaders and members went underground, reorganized in the *maquis*, and increased their petitions.

An anomaly within the general historiography of political petitioning, UPC, JDC, and UDEFEC petitions did not influence legislation in the process of nation-state building. Instead of promoting the inclusion of petitioners in the political process, for members of the UPC, UDEFEC, and the JDC, the high volume of petitions coincided with their total exclusion from the formation of their nation's government. The petitions fell on deaf ears in the Trusteeship Council, although Eastern bloc and non-Western members such as the USSR and India supported the Cameroonian nationalists. The majority of Trusteeship Council and General Assembly representatives repeatedly voted to support French and British efforts to suppress the nationalist movement and failed to respond to Cameroonian nationalists' requests for a UN appointed international supervisory coalition to oversee

---

[16] Janvier Onana, *Le sacre des indigènes évolués: essai sur la professionalisation politique (l'exemple du cameroun)*, Paris, 2004, 228.
[17] At the 21st Session, 30 January to 26 March 1956, the Committee adopted this new procedure, making it more difficult to gauge the exact number of petitions, as well as the identity and geographical location of the senders.

elections beginning in 1956.[18] Yet despite the UN's lack of response, the act of petitioning contributed immeasurably to the creation of popular nationalism in Cameroon, allowing the movement to outgrow its leadership and to expand beyond the borders of Cameroonian territory.

The petitions from Cameroonian women offer a rare written source for the voices of African women involved in the political process.[19] The petitions can be divided by chronological periods. During the first period, pre 1954, the leaders' formal petitions employed sophisticated language that matched the new ideology of human rights represented by the UN, and fledgling NGOs. During this stage, leaders of the nationalist movement claimed their right to appeal to the international authority of the UN, thus integrating Cameroonian nationalism into a wider international movement for human rights and self-determination.

During the second phase, late 1954 through 1956, tensions between the French administration and the "progressive" parties are increasingly visible in the petitions, eventually culminating in the French ban of UPC, JDC, and UDEFEC parties. During this phase, petitioners reacted against the repressive nature of foreign administration, pointing out the inconsistencies between the UN's purpose (to protect inhabitants of trust territories) and the French administration's arbitrary arrest and punishment of

---

[18] The UPC continued to request UN supervision of political processes such as elections and the formation of legislative bodies until Cameroon's independence in 1960.

[19] The studies of women's involvement in African nationalist politics rely primarily on contemporary interviews. See Geiger, *TANU Women*, and Nina Emma Mba, *Nigerian Women Mobilized: Women's Political Activity in Southern Nigeria, 1900-1965*, Berkeley, 1982, chap. 8. In Geiger and Mba's studies of women in nationalist politics, references to interviews outnumber by far references to women's writings.

nationalists. There was a marked increase in petitions from individuals who expressed private grievances in terms that linked them to popular nationalist rhetoric. Petitioners exposed incidents of repression that they suffered at the hands of a harmful foreign regime, and extrapolated from them reasons for claiming independence for the whole population.

Finally, after 1956, both British and French administrations spared nothing to eradicate the movement. Cameroonians lived under military occupation that was particularly heavy in the Bamileke and Sanaga-Maritime regions. UPC, UDEFEC and JDC leaders were forced into exile, and the act of petitioning was severely punished. The outlawed nationalist movement was now completely outside the sphere of official politics, but in this phase the petitions were most numerous as petitioners made a last, desperate appeal to the UN, and reproached it for its refusal to come to their aid.

Petitions on an International Scale: Some Comparisons with other Trusteeships

Petitions from trusteeship territories marked the emergence of African discussions of politics and nationalism within an international forum, uncensored by European administrators. Africans in the trusteeship territories addressed an international supervisory body beyond the confines of the governing administration, suggesting that petitioners tapped into a dawning international moral order of human rights. The Trusteeship Council records contain numerous petitions from African trusteeship territories such as the British and French Cameroons, Togoland, French

Togo, Tanganyika, South West Africa (Namibia), Ruanda-Urundi, and Somalia, particularly during the 1950s.

In most cases, the historiography of African nationalism lacks a thorough analysis of the trusteeship petitions. Zedekia Ngavirue mentions petitions to the Trusteeship Council conceived of and circulated by Herero Chief Kutako in Namibia, rejecting the establishment of South Africa as Administering Authority in August 1947. For Ngavirue, Chief Kutako was the "chief inspirer and leader of the post-war resistance movement which became the main source of modern nationalism."[20] Ngavirue does not reveal the content of the petitions, nor does he discuss the significance of the act of petitioning itself. The Herero resistance movement against South Africa, waged within the territory of South West Africa, contributed to the dawning of Namibian nationalism, but Ngavirue fails to articulate the way in which the tenuous links between local and international politics formed during the process.

Somali political parties employed petitions following international discussion of Somalia's future administrative status at the UN. The Somali Youth League was formed in 1948 to fight against the establishment of an Italian Trust Administration, and Abdullahi Issa appeared before the Trusteeship Council to express his party's opposition. At the same time, the pro-Italian Conferenza delta Somalia sent a delegate to the Trusteeship Council to demonstrate the people's support of the trusteeship arrangements. Both the northern-based Somali Youth League and the southern-based Conferenza delta Somalia claimed to represent a majority of

---

[20]Zedekia Ngavirue, *Political Parties and Interest Groups in South West Africa (Namibia}: A Study of a Plural Society*, Basel, Switzerland, 1997, 181, 183.

the population.[21] A myriad other political parties also sprang up during this period, many of which addressed petitions to the Trusteeship Council. These petitions in the Trusteeship Council records have yet to be evaluated to ascertain their role in the formation of Somalian nationalism.

Two historians deal in greater depth with petitions from local populations of Tanganyika to the UN, although in isolated cases. Thomas Spear focuses on the petitions sent during the Meru land case in 1951 in his study of Meru and Arusha access to land in colonial Tanganyika.[22] Spear suggests that, although the Meru lost their case before the UN in 1952 and 1953, the act of petitioning galvanized a collective political consciousness that coincided with rejection of colonialism. For the Meru and the Arusha, the colonial settlers' appropriation of land, particularly when not cultivated, demonstrated the immorality of the colonial administration. The Meru land case thus precipitated a growing discussion of local and national politics in Tanganyika, in matters ranging from the structure of local government and chieftainships, to subsequent land disputes and regulation of coffee cultivation. Eventually the Meru land case sparked a rejection of colonial ideology and authority, and evolved into "a rallying cry for the nationalist movement in Tanganyika."[23]

Steven Feierman discusses petitions from the Usambara Citizens Union in Tanganyika.[24] Feierman's analysis of the UCU's use of petitions sheds light on the party's

[21] Robert L. Hess, *Italian Colonialism in Somalia,* Chicago, 1966, 191-2.

[22] Thomas Spear, *Mountain Farmers: Moral Economies of Land and Agricultural Development in Arusha and Meru,* Berkeley, 1997. See especially chap. 11.

[23] Ibid., 191, 193, 209, 229-30, 234.

[24] Steven Feierman, *Peasant Intellectuals: Anthropology and History in Tanzania,* Madison, 1990.

differentiation between written and spoken ideology. In Feierman's analysis, the UCU deliberately omitted issues – such as rainmaking and chiefly authority – from petitions addressed to the Trusteeship Council. Feierman surmises that UCU leaders probably knew that "it was inappropriate and counterproductive to write to London or New York about healing the land," even though this was an issue that Shambaa peasant intellectuals believed to be at the crux of their moral and political economy. [25] The "politics of rain" were "discussed in Shambaa, not Swahili or English, a subject discussed among neighbors in informal conversation ... in spoken language, not in writing."[26] On paper, then, the UCU did not openly challenge the British administration, and unlike Nyerere's TANU movement, did not question the legitimacy of colonial government. Although the UCU petitions constituted an appeal to the UN whose intervention might have influenced local politics, Shambaa did not insert UN policies into their local discussions of rainmaking and chiefship. Instead, they upheld a separation between local and international political discourses. The UCU's relationship to the UN thus differed from the UPC's, which, as we shall see below, diffused UN ideology throughout the territory until villagers and rural populations clamored for copies of the Universal Declaration of Human Rights at local meetings.

These case studies suggest a link between politics at the grassroots level and African trust territory inhabitants' growing awareness of international politics and the UN's promotion of autonomy. African petitioners consciously took advantage of opportunities provided by international observation (displayed most visibly by the UN Visiting

---

[25] Ibid., 210 and chap. 8.
[26] Ibid., 210.

Mission) to advocate for their political causes. Inhabitants of trusteeship territories, once they had learned of an outside authority to whom they could appeal, claimed international attention for their local problems, fueling their own political fervor in the process, although this fervor was expressed differently from place to place. In some territories local politicians appealed to the UN within the context of their own small locale, while in others, and such is the case of the UPC, consciousness of the UN galvanized a nationalist movement.

The act of petitioning shaped and guided the UPC ideology and fostered its popularity. The UDEFEC, UPC, and JDC petitioners combined local grievances, party ideology, and an increasing international awareness to create a popular anti-colonial narrative. This narrative was structured and passed along through the very act of petitioning at regional and local UPC, UDEFEC and JDC meetings. When UPC and UDEFEC leaders met with local Cameroonians an ideological hybridization occurred, between international and local, the political and the personal, leaders and followers, the literate and the illiterate, urban and rural, men and women. At local meetings, UDEFEC leaders read aloud Ruben Um Nyobé's speeches to the UN. They read the Universal Declaration of Human Rights and the UN Charter and told the story of the formation of UDEFEC. The leaders then encouraged those attending to give back their own stories, to articulate them in the form of a petition, and to sign their name to the struggle for independence and unification, thus perpetuating a nationalist narrative.

Narrative, Language, and Literacy

Focusing on the petitions from UDEFEC raises issues of literacy, language, and the authenticity of petitioners' narratives. Despite Cameroon's comparatively high level of literacy, literacy rates were lowest among women.[27] In 1927, there were only two hundred women in schools in French Cameroon - and women's interest in politics had been discouraged, both by Cameroonian males and by the French administration. [28] The UDEFEC petitions tell us how its women members organized politically, by establishing networks between the educated urban leaders of UDEFEC and the rural areas in which women would otherwise have had little concept of nationhood or trusteeship status.

For example, in 1954, the leaders of UDEFEC in Douala, Emma Mbem, Marie-Irène Ngapeth, Marthe Ouandié, and Marie Meïdo, petitioned the UN for the release of Pierre Penda, a UPC activist and member of Solidarité Babimbi (an association promoting the economic development of the region).[29] Two months later his wife, Marthe Penda, Secretary of the Babimbi branch of UDEFEC, wrote on behalf of the "women of Babimbi," to denounce the lack of infrastructure in the region, and request that her husband be set free.[30] The

---

[27] On the history of Cameroonian literacy and education, see Bjornson, chap. 2.

[28] Chantal Ndami, "La dynamique de la participation des femmes a la vie politique: le cas du Parlement camerounais, 1960-1997," MA Thesis, Université de Yaoundé-I, 1997, chap. 1. I thank Professor Odile Chatap-Ekindi for bringing Ndami's thesis to my attention.

[29] Petition from the Office of UDEFEC concerning the Cameroons under French Administration, 1 Oct 1954, Trusteeship Council, T/PET.5/365.

[30] Petition from the Babimbi branch of UDEFEC, 13 Dec 1954, Trusteeship Council, T/PET.5/.409 and Petition from Mrs. Marthe

leaders of UDEFEC, based in Douala, supported the women of Babimbi in making claims for the economic advancement of the region and for the release of political prisoner Pierre Penda. The incident thus strengthened the link between Babimbi members of the UPC and UDEFEC and the Douala leaders.

The combination of UDEFEC petitions with the few remaining records of local UDEFEC meetings in the Babimbi region and interviews with surviving members of UDEFEC point to the creation of a new narrative that became instrumental in creating and spreading nationalist ideas across regions at the grassroots. I suggest that the reason for the widespread dissemination of the UPC message came from the combination of oral transmission with written distribution. The structure of the party - local committee meetings at the grassroots level, linked by traveling delegations that read UPC and UN documents aloud at the local meetings - enabled the UPC's nationalist platform to take root in its "stabilized form."[31] For example, the official account of UDEFEC's origin in 1952 was told and retold at local meetings in the Babimbi region three or four years later, but the account varied somewhat from meeting to meeting,

---

Penda, Secretary of UDEFEC, Babimbi, 21 Jan 1955, T/PET.5/409/Add. l.

[31] Jan Vansina, *Oral Tradition as History*, Madison, 1985, 17. Stabilized form refers to an account of an event which, once told and retold, begins to conform to a set rendition. For Vansina, this stabilized form is achieved after the account of events has been transmitted "for a generation or so." I am suggesting that when the account is narrated through a combination of oral and written transmission, the stabilized form is achieved more rapidly. A written version existed against which the account could be verified, but the oral transmission that took place at local meetings and between UPC and UDEFEC members still allowed for the type of variation consistent with the genres of "historical gossip," "group account," and "hearsay" described in Vansina's chap. 1.

19

according to who recounted the event, who recorded it and how. Certainly, if the same account were retold at local meetings in the Bamileke region, regional variations could be expected. Thus, although the UPC message and the official account of the party's formation were standardized in written form, the party's popularity arose out of the widespread oral distribution of information about the party. This distribution occurred primarily through oral accounts, hearsay, gossip, and rumor - means of information exchange available to non-literate populations. The mandatory presence of a literate scribe at every meeting ensured the transfer of ideas from their oral form to the written documents of meeting minutes and petitions.

Um Nyobé understood the importance of these two means of transmitting the party message. A prolific writer himself,[32] he advocated use of the written word to record the party's history, to inform the UN of abuses faced by the nationalists,[33] and to provide prisoners' written descriptions of incarceration in the French administration's prisons. He also emphasized the role of the UPC as educator of the people, and established a school, *L'Ecole des cadres*, for the education of party leaders. After the party was banned, the initiative to educate future leaders continued underground.[34] Nevertheless, recognizing the importance of word of mouth to convey information, and not wanting the party message to be available only to the mostly urban educated and literate members, he stressed the importance of local committees in facilitating the oral transmission of the party message. The

---

[32] Many of the writings and speeches of Ruben Um Nyobé have been compiled in two volumes edited by Achille Mbembe: *Problème National Kamerunais*, Paris, 1984, and *Ecrits Sous Maquis*, Paris, 1989.

[33] Um Nyobé, *Problème*, 160-172.

[34] Um Nyobé, *Ecrits*, 210-212.

women of UDEFEC played a key role in this transmission (Chapter 3), by using skits, songs, stories, and even biblical parables, to convey party objectives.

The UDEFEC petitions constitute a genre consistent with oral transmission that is then committed to writing.[35] The act of writing down individuals' spoken accounts promoted the diffusion of stories about UDEFEC and UPC members on a national scale, eventually permitting their stories to reach the international audience of the Trusteeship Council. The petitionary genre's collective meaning holds greater significance than the individual petition.[36] Throughout the process of petitioning, individual complaints against the colonial administration contributed to a growing collection of such stories, which in turn established the bedrock of "ideas on which experience can be based."[37] Individuals committed their stories to writing in the form of petitions, which were sometimes used as illustrations in the party's tracts that were then circulated and read aloud at meetings. The personal nature of these stories encouraged more stories to be shared,

---

[35] Ibid., 218-221.

[36] See Luise White, *Speaking with Vampires: Rumor and History in Colonial Africa*, Berkeley, 1999, chap. 8, for a discussion of vernacular newspapers in 1950s Uganda as providing another venue for the transmission of rumors, which challenges the separation of oral and written narratives in the historiography. White explores stories of vampires and blood-sucking in East and Central Africa by focusing on the stories' generic and formulaic qualities rather than on their specificity and accuracy in narrating isolated events. The vampire stories gained credibility through their diffuse transmission by way of gossip, indicating "a claim to knowledge and the right to speak it." White, *Vampires*, 65. Moreover, gossip forms links between gossipers and extends those links from the transmitter of information to the community at larger, or the state. Gossip and the circulation of rumors can facilitate the formation of a community identity as well as delineate the standards and beliefs adhered to by that community. See also Vansina, 17-18.

[37] White, *Vampires*, 33.

allowing members to identify with people outside their own locale, whom they may never have met. Through this exchange, the UPC message and ideology became personalized and more widely credible.[38]

The act of recording the stories in the form of written petitions lent even greater credibility to the UPC. When the stories of an individual were written down and transmitted to meetings throughout the territory in the form of a petition that could be signed onto, a personal grievance became fodder for the nationalist cause. In some cases, particularly when members were shot by the French or British administration, the names of the victims became known as martyrs throughout a larger region. When Irenée Taffo and his pregnant wife were shot in Mankon (near Bamenda), petitioners from Bamenda to Kumba cited the incident in their petitions as an example of French and British collaboration in disciplining UPC members in exile from the French territory.[39]

It is impossible to verify the historical accuracy of the individual petitions, although much of the information they contain can be corroborated. Their verifiable accuracy is not the main point here, however. Reading the petitions together, it is possible to piece together the emergence of an anti-colonial, pro-independence nationalism created, popularized, and disseminated through the act of petitioning.

---

[38] Ibid.: "It is through talking that people learn about cause and intention."

[39] See Petition from the UPK concerning the Cameroons under British administration, Bamenda, 4 April 1957, T/PET.4/126 and T/PET.4/126/Add. l; Kumba, 6 April 1957; T/PET.4/127; Petition from the Bamenda Central Committee, 5 April 1957, T/PET.4/128, Petition from the Azare Local Committee, 8 April 1957, T/PET.4/129; Petition from Mr. Gregory Kang, Abokpa, 4 April 1957, T/PET.4/131.

Sources and methodology

The Trusteeship Council petitions provide the richest source of information for UDEFEC's history and role in the UPC's ideological and popular evolution. Because of the new procedure for processing the petitions that the Trusteeship Council adopted in 1956, beginning in that year the record shows the number of petitions sent from each village rather than documenting the names, locations, and exact dates of each petition's origin. As such, the precise number of petitions sent by women nationalists remains unknown. On the average, the ratio of women's petitions to men's was about 1 to 6. Since more than 45,000 petitions poured into the Trusteeship Council from Cameroonian nationalists from 1956 to 1960, it seems a likely estimate that at least 7,000 of the nationalist petitions from the Cameroons were sent by women. Like the petitions from the UPC, petitions sent by women nationalists increased, spiking in 1956, the year after the party's ban in French Cameroon, and again in 1958, the year of the last UN Visiting Mission to the Cameroons. While many of the petitions were from UDEFEC committees, at least 162 of those sent by women came from individuals who identified themselves by name. One-hundred-and-eight of these women identified themselves further, either by occupation, marital status, or otherwise. It is important to note that, after agriculturalist, the majority of individual petitioners identified themselves as an officer of UDEFEC or One Kamerun, [40] suggesting the significance of this role for Cameroonian women nationalists. A number of women

---

[40] From late 1955, UPC, UDEFEC and JDC members employed the German spelling, "Kamerun," to indicate their desire for a unified territory.

indicated that they were widows, particularly those whose husbands had been killed during the nationalist struggle.

In Yaoundé, I read the few remaining UPC and UDEFEC files in the *Archives Nationales de Yaoundé* (ANY). Um Nyobé encouraged leaders to keep copious records of meeting minutes, and the names and places of origin of those attending. He wanted proof of the party's popularity to bring before the UN, and he wished to promote members' historical consciousness that came with active record-keeping. Record-keeping also proved a way to monitor the local meetings' activities and enable visiting Central or Regional leaders to make evaluations of the meetings' growth and progress. During the French administration's occupation of the Sanaga-Maritime beginning in 1957, referred to as the *Zone de Pacification du Cameroun* (ZOPAC), the seizure of these documents in the homes of UPC and UDEFEC members was a key part of the French administration's strategy to uproot the movement.[41] Likewise, in the British region, after the party was outlawed, the administration prioritized the confiscation of meeting records and printed tracts. Although many of these records remained in Yaoundé and were eventually classified in ANY, many of the files are missing, even when they are catalogued as part of ANY's collection. Among the missing files are the records of UDEFEC's activity in Douala. Nevertheless, there was a voluminous file of UDEFEC records from Babimbi, from 1955-1957. This file enabled me to understand the organization of local meetings in the Babimbi region during a period of increasingly violent repression of the movement by the

---

[41] Marc Michel, "Une décolonisation confisquée? Perspectives sur la décolonisation du Cameroun sous tutelle de la France 1955-1960," *Revue française d'histoire d'Outre-mer* 324-324 (1999): 221-258.

French administration. Mostly handwritten, sometimes in Bassa, these documents contain meeting minutes; members' names, occupations, and villages of origin; the names of the meetings' scribes; and rates of membership fees. These documents thus provide the backdrop for the creation of UDEFEC's petitions to the UN.

While in Cameroon during the summer of 1999, I had the opportunity to interview members of UDEFEC from the pre-independence period, namely Marie-Irène Ngapeth-Biyong who served as General-Secretary during the 1950s. In 1999, and again in 2001, 2002, and 2003, I also interviewed Marcel Ngandjong Feze, *Fo* (chief) of Bandenkop, who was instated as a pro-UPC chief in 1955, at age 18, only to be forced into exile shortly thereafter. I spoke with the children of UPC and UDEFEC members from the period, who remember the arrests of their parents and prefer not to be named. Although the UPC and UDEFEC officially reorganized as an opposition party following the democratic opening of 1990, many of the members believe that they still risk persecution from the government and prefer to keep a low profile. These interviews, although sparse, provided me with oral material to fill in the gaps from the written records available.

The tracts and booklets published by UPC leaders in exile comprised the fourth variety of source material I consulted. This literature was distributed internationally by such foreign delegations as the Bureau of Leading Committee of the Union of the Populations of Cameroon, headed by Félix Moumié and Ernest Ouandié, based in Cairo.[42] The publisher

---

[42] See, for example, UPC, *The UPC Denounces the Planned Systematic Tortures in the Kamerun,* Cairo, 1958; UPC, *La tutelle internationale a l'épreuve,* Cairo,

of these tracts in Cairo had links with the Afro-Asian Solidarity movement, and the literature put forth by the UPC emphasized Cameroon's place in the international struggle for independence from global Western dominance.[43] Numerous newspapers published by the UPC, the JDC, and UDEFEC during the period were sold to increase UPC funds locally, but often only a few issues were printed per title. These newspapers included, *L'Etoile*, *Lumière*, *L'Opinion au Cameroun*, *Le Travailleur Camerounais* (USCC), *La Voix du Cameroun*, and *Femmes Camerounaises* (UDEFEC). These newspapers have yet to be evaluated in a systematic way to analyze the evolving ideology of the UPC, along with the links or fissures between the leaders who stayed behind underground, and those writing from exile. These publications contained UPC party messages: the Joint Proclamation of April 1955, for instance, was published in *La Voix du Cameroun* and in *Femmes Camerounaises*. The newspapers also contained copies of Ruben Um Nyobé's speeches at UPC Congresses or before the General Assembly at the UN, or copies of petitions sent to the UN.

Finally I used contemporary UDEFEC publications, which contain the official history of the party as written by Marie-Irène Ngapeth-Biyong, President of the reformed UDEFEC party. These documents tell the official history of the faction of the party that survived underground in post-

---

1959. Achille Mbembe attributes these writings to Félix Moumié. Mbembe, "Introduction," in Um Nyobé, *Maquis*, 17.

[43] See, for example, UPC, *From Algeria to the Kamerun*, Cairo, [1958?]; Meredith Terretta, "Cameroonian Nationalists Go Global: From Forest *Maquis* to a Pan-African Accra," *Journal of African History* 51.2 (2010): 189–212; Matthew Connelly, *A Diplomatic Revolution: Algeria's Fight for Independence and the Origins of the Post–Cold War Era*, Oxford: Oxford University Press, 2002.

colonial Cameroon. The diverse sources allow the researcher to piece together a party history by combining individual accounts and official party records. In recent years both Marie-Irène Ngapeth-Biyong and Marthe Moumié published their memoirs.[44] Fortunately they completed these works just before their deaths. These works have served to fill in the context and contours of this history.

The UPC formed as a popular party, to advocate for the rights of Cameroonians within the international sphere of the UN. In Chapter 2, I discuss the party's origins, starting from its trade union foundations protesting forced labor in post-war Douala. This burgeoning labor initiative was fueled by international influences, such as the release of the UN Charter, the arrival of French *Confédération Générale du Travail* labor organizers, and the formation of the *Rassemblement Démocratique Africain*. To prove the popularity of the party he represented at the General Assembly, Ruben Um Nyobé stressed the importance of grassroots organization, i.e.: the formation of local committees. At the same time, he encouraged the involvement of women in the party. In the increasingly politicized urban environment of post-war Yaoundé and Douala, women recognized and responded to an opportunity to advocate for their own rights and those of their children. UDEFEC was born of these circumstances in post-war Cameroon, growing out of Um Nyobé's initiative to popularize UPC ideology. UDEFEC responded to the social and economic desires of Cameroonian women at the time, and Chapter 2 outlines the link between the UPC, UDEFEC, and its larger place in the international sphere.

---

[44] Marie-Irène Ngapeth-Biyong, *Cameroun: Combats pour l'indépendance*, Paris, 2009; Marthe Moumié, *Victime du colonialisme français: Mon mari Félix Moumié*, Paris, 2006.

Gradually, UDEFEC women began to conceive of their socio-economic claims in political terms, as the UPC and UDEFEC increased in size and strength and the French administration attempted to stifle its popularity. Chapter 3 explores the political coming of age of UDEFEC members, as their ideology evolved from claiming rights for themselves and their families, to rejecting the colonial order that they began to recognize as the source of their oppression. At the same time, their use of petitions increased, particularly after the French administration banned the parties by decree on 13 July 1955. Thereafter, women approached the UN to plead the causes of their husbands who faced harassment, harsh beatings, imprisonment, and death. Chapter 4 explains the transformation of the personal grievances felt by UDEFEC women into a political outcry on the national level. The party quickly reorganized underground, in the *maquis* in the Sanaga-Maritime, Mungo and Bamileke regions, and through the official delegation at Kumba, in British territory. Chapter 4 explains how reorganization underground and in exile from French Cameroon enabled UDEFEC to take root even more firmly in these particular locales.

UDEFEC's rejection of the colonial order in rural regions occurred in areas of specific concern to women, particularly in medicine, birthing practices, and agricultural practices. The women of UDEFEC attempted to reclaim the social well-being of their communities by eradicating the influence of European administrators and missionaries from these areas. In Chapter 5, I argue that UDEFEC women in rural areas had begun to perceive the European presence, even within the institutions of churches and dispensaries, as pernicious to the collective good of Cameroonian society. The petitions became a way to write the Europeans out of Cameroonian society, at least in the nationalist collective imaginary.

Chapter 6 explores the effects of the total exclusion of UPC nationalists from the formation of the nation's government. Even after the British followed the French in banning the UPC, the JDC, and UDEFEC from its territory in 1957 and the leaders were forced into exile (although Ruben Um Nyobé and a band of his followers hid in the *maquis*), the party continued to rain petitions upon the UN. Foreign factions of exiled members and their international sympathizers continued to support the party insofar as possible from outside the borders of the territory. The nature of the "Civil War" in the Bamileke region has yet to be fully explored,[45] as does the strength of the party throughout the territory, and the role of exiled members in supporting *maquisards* materially and otherwise. Even in the last years of the trusteeship period, the movement maintained a visible appearance of cohesion and unified ideology within the UN petitions, suggesting that the movement had outgrown dependence on its leaders and taken on a life of its own. Tragically, without the guidance of the leadership as foundation, many petitioners remained unaware of significant events, such as Um Nyobé's assassination on 13 September 1958, and the end of the UN's trust administration on 14 March 1959. The Conclusion attempts to account for the popular survival of the UPC, UDEFEC, and JDC, even after the fragmentation of its leadership, and emphasizes some of these unresolved questions.

---

[45] But see Thomas Deltombe, et al, *Kamerun: Une guerre cachée aux origines de la Françafrique (1948–1971)*, Paris, 2011 and Meredith Terretta, *Nation of Outlaws, State of Violence: Nationalism, Grassfields Tradition and State-Building in Cameroon*, Athens, OH, forthcoming 2013.

In taking up this project, I hoped that its primary purpose would be to demonstrate how much of the UPC, UDEFEC, and JDC's history remains unexplored. Several studies in UPC historiography offer explanations of UPC nationalism that can not stand up under close scrutiny: that the UPC was primarily a Communist movement, that it was a primarily based in the Sanaga-Maritime, that it terrorized the Cameroonian population,[46] and that "social cadets" in the Bamileke region used its name to overturn the traditional hierarchy of their elders[47] are but a few of these questionable conclusions. I hope that by approaching UPC ideology and history through the women's movement, UDEFEC, enough questions surface about the history of this revolutionary nationalist movement to encourage further scholarship.

---

[46] Michel, "Décolonisation," 229-258.

[47] Bayart, *Cameroun*.

Chapter 2

Ruben Um Nyobé and the Multi-Layered Origins of the UPC And UDEFEC

"Women have the same rights as men, and can no longer be kept on one side when it is a question of the political, economic, social, and cultural interests of their country."

-Petition from the *Comité Féminin de l'UPC* concerning the Cameroons under French and British Administration, 20 November 1949.

In post-war Cameroon, a mosaic of organizations spread throughout the territory, prompted by the swirling influences of economics, traditional governance, changes in France's government, trade unionism, and the presence of French communists.[1] Out of this mosaic, the UPC took shape in April 1948, containing strains of many of the organizations that had preceded it, including the USCC, the traditional associations of the Duala and Bamileke notables, Ngondo[2]

---

[1] Richard Joseph, "Nationalism in Postwar Cameroon: The Difficult Birth of the UPC," *Journal of African Studies* 2.2 (1975): 201-29 details the organization of these various groups. The French communists, such as Gaston Donnat (who served as the first secretary-general of the USCC) not only supported the organization of labor and trade unions, but also helped to organize the *Cercles d'études sociales et syndicales* in Yaoundé and Douala, which attracted young intellectuals, eager to discuss their country's future. Richard A. Joseph, *Radical Nationalism in Cameroun: Social Origins of the UPC Rebellion*, Oxford: Clarendon Press, 1977, 57.

[2] Ngondo, the Traditional Assembly of the Duala Peoples, was made up of young Duala intelligentsia and traditional Duala chiefs. In 1945, Ngondo submitted a memorandum entitled "Avis à toute la Population

and Kumsze,[3] respectively, and the pan-African alliance of Leftist political parties, the *Rassemblement Démocratique Africain* (RDA).[4] The UPC's ideology drew upon the intellectual precedent established by parties advocating for the autonomy of Cameroon in all arenas from the political to the economic.[5] These parties veered away from the

---

du Cameroun (Noire et Blanche)" that expressed its militantly anti-colonial sentiments, opposing the French intent to assimilate French Cameroon into the French Union, and attacking those Cameroonians who tried to further this goal in exchange for monetary or political benefits. See Joseph, *Radical Nationalism*, 78-9, 82, 175-6.

[3] Kumsze, the Tradition Association of the Bamileke Peoples, was an association of Bamileke notables who rejected colonialism in favor of what they described as "traditional" Bamileke forms of government. One of their main objectives was to restore the delegation of Bamileke chiefs by their own people, rather than having them selected by the French administration. Kumsze's claims for independence were also prompted in large part by the desire of Bamileke planters to be free of the French administration's restrictions on coffee growing. Djoumessi's popularity and leadership came after he ignored the French administration's regulations of coffee growing and distributed seeds to "unauthorized" farmers. See Ndobegang M. Mbapndah, "French Colonial Agricultural Policy, African Chiefs, and Coffee Growing in the Cameroun Grassfields, 1920-1960," *The International Journal of African Historical Studies* 27 (1994): 41-58.

[4] Five "unofficial" Cameroonian delegates had attended the Bamako Congress in October 1946, at which RDA leaders from French West Africa encouraged the formation of territorial branches of the RDA throughout Africa under French administration. Cameroonian representatives included: Ruben Um Nyobé, trade unionist, Djoumessi Mathias, the Chief of Dschang and leader of Kumzse, and Celestin Takala, a Bamileke merchant based in Douala who sought to defend the financial interests of Cameroonian business men from French price controls. For Um Nyobé's role in the Bamako Congress, see Mortimer, 125; for Takala's role in Cameroonian politics, see Joseph, "Birth," 207.

[5] The earliest non-Francophile parties that formed in post-war Cameroon were the *Mouvement démocratique Camerounais*, formed in 1945 and led by a Duala trade unionist, Léopold Moumé-Etia, and the *Front Intercolonial*, a pan-African organization based in Paris, of which a Cameroonian section, organized by war veterans and ex-servicemen who had spent time in the

32

"Francophile"[6] tendency displayed by the few parties formed during the inter-war period with the support of the French administration. The RDA, combined with trade union organization and the presence of French socialists and communists such as Gaston Donnat who worked to set up the *Cercles d'études sociales et syndicales* in Yaoundé and Douala contributed to the intellectual content of the UPC's platform.

On 10 April 1948, twelve men who had been active participants in postwar political discussions gathered in front of a small bar in the Wouri region just outside Douala.[7] Their objective was to piece together a cohesive nationalist movement that appealed to the greatest number of Cameroonians throughout the territory. The struggles each of them brought to the discussion (such as the demand for higher wages and better working conditions; the right for all farmers to cultivate cash crops; and the lifting of price controls and export laws favoring the *colons* – or colonial settlers) represented the diversity of anti-colonial sentiment among Cameroonians. The UPC brought these issues

---

metropole, was officially recognized on 8 July 1946. See Joseph, "Birth," 206-207.

[6] Joseph uses this term to describe those parties whose leaders sought to reap the gains extended by the French administration to *évolués*, usually by supporting the formation of a French Union of territories under French administration. See Joseph, "Birth," 206.

[7] The identity of those present at this initial gathering is not clear. It is probable that among them were representatives of Kumsze, Ngondo, the USCC, those who had attended the RDA congress in Bamako and the former RACAM (see fn 9, below). Ruben Um Nyobé, who had already caught the attention of French administrators for his trade-unionist activities, kept a low profile at the party's inception preferring to allow Leonard Bouly, a civil servant who provided little threat to the French administration, to serve as General-Secretary. See Achille Mbembe, "Introduction," in Um Nyobé, *Problème national kamerunais*, Paris, 1984, and Joseph, "Birth," 218-21.

together and recast them in an effort to democratize Cameroon and emancipate "the people exploited by colonial firms."[8] By the time of Ruben Um Nyobé's assassination in September 1958, UPC ideology had evolved from the struggle against European economic domination to a total rejection of colonial administration on every level ranging from the economic, to the cultural, to the political. Although he kept a low profile during the UPC's formation, Ruben Um Nyobé was the main strategist behind the scenes, and his speeches and writings a major source of its passion, dedication, and popularity.

On 9 June 1948, the French administration officially acknowledged receipt of the UPC's statutes, and the UPC held its first public meeting as an official party on 22 June 1946 at the *Salle des Fêtes d'Akwa* in Douala with five hundred people in attendance. [9] From its inception, the UPC demonstrated a character of political inclusiveness, consciously structured to avoid the ethnic divisions and personal opportunism that had caused the downfalls of other parties.[10] The opening phrase of the UPC constitution read:

---

[8] Rapports de Sûreté, 27 Dec 1947 - 3 Jan 1948, as quoted in Joseph, "Birth," 218.

[9] Joseph, "Birth," 222-23. UPC organizers had learned from the administration's hostile response to the first RDA-affiliated party, the *Rassemblement Camerounais* (RACAM), whose constitution the French administration simply refused to recognize. This underscored the importance of the "politics of registration" for nationalist parties in dealing with the administration, and the UPC's formation demonstrated the political savvy of those who had learned from experience. For RACAM's formation and the French administration's subsequent intimidation of those involved, see ibid., 213-15.

[10] Um Nyobé had written to Félix Moumié, a doctor employed by the administration, that he wished to avoid a Duala-centric party, suggesting that this had been another reason for RACAM's rapid dissolution. Joseph, "Birth," 223.

"In Cameroon, there has been created a movement whose goal is to bring together and unite the inhabitants of this territory in order to bring about a more rapid evolution of the population and the increase in their standard of living." The inclusion of women was compatible with the UPC's political character of promoting popular participation.

The Organization of Cameroonian Women in Collaboration with the UPC

As early as 1945, Cameroonian women had begun to organize in postwar Cameroon as well, responding to the same socio-economic and political currents swirling through Yaoundé and Douala. Although a handful of different women's parties formed in the early 1950s, [11] the UPC provided the most dynamic and significant role for Cameroonian women in politics, encouraging the formation of a women's wing, UDEFEC, which, although in support of the UPC, would enjoy autonomy in organization and in funding. However, even before the official formation of UDEFEC in 1952, the *Comité féminin de l'UPC* composed the first petition from women on record at the Trusteeship Council.

The *Comité féminin de l'UPC* explicitly justified women's entrance into formal politics in the opening paragraph of their 1949 petition:

> *Convinced that we are expressing the profound sentiments of the great majority of our women compatriots; considering that women have the same rights as men, and can no longer be kept on one side when it is a question of the political, economic, social and cultural*

---

[11] These included the *Association des femmes de l'Union française au Cameroun* formed in Douala on 17 Sept 1949 and the *Union des femmes camerounaises.*

interests of their country; considering that Cameroonian women are victims of a policy of contempt aimed at keeping them always in a state of inferiority...[12]

Laying the groundwork for women's participation in politics, the *comité féminin* protested against forced labor and the *indigénat* because these policies caused "displacement and separation of families."[13] They denounced the policy of racial discrimination faced daily by Cameroonian women who "have no right to get served ... before white women and their servants," in the shops.[14] They expressed concerns about the lack of health care resulting in high rates of infant mortality, and decried the shortage of schools, "condemning our children to ignorance."[15]

Emphasizing education for women, the petition stated that "the women of Cameroon have the right and duty to take part in the work of emancipating our country," and the "lack of education constitutes a serious obstacle to the

---

[12] Petition from the Comité féminin de l'UPC concerning the Cameroons under French and British administration, 20 Nov 1949, UNTC, T/PET.4/32.

[13] Although the *indigénat* (the practice of arbitrarily sentencing indigenous inhabitants of territories under French administration to fines to be paid in labor, or prison terms including forced labor) had been dismantled by a decree of 20 February 1946, and forced labor abolished by a bill passed on 11 April 1946, these changes in policy proved difficult to enforce. See Mortimer, 67, 74-76. The UPC continued to protest against the administration's use of prisoners to perform arduous labor. See for example, "Régime pénitentaire des détenus politiques (UPC) à la prison de Yaoundé, 1955," 1 AC 1977, ANY. Petitions also referred to the use of schoolboys in the Catholic missions to perform labor tasks for priests as forced labor. See Petition from the General Assembly of the UPC held at Bafang, 5 Dec 1954, T/PET.5/410.

[14] T/PET.4/32.

[15] Ibid.

prospects" of them doing so.[16] These claims would surface again and again in UDEFEC petitions after the party's formation in 1952.

The UPC's willing inclusion of a *comité féminin* at this time demonstrated its democratic and multi-regional character, later summarized in *La voix du Cameroun*:

> *We call without hesitation for a union of Africans, men and women, of all classes, tribes, religions and viewpoints. But our union ... is based on an ideal which must be common to all these persons who ... suffer from colonialist oppression. The union should therefore have as its one condition: the struggle against colonialism.*[17]

In contrast, ESOCAM, formed with the French administration's support to oppose the UPC,[18] developed a policy towards women that was as conservative as its pro-

---

[16] Ibid. Until 1948 Cameroonian women did not attend French schools, however, after 1948, the French began to encourage education for the daughters of *évolués* in urban centers such as Dschang, Garoua, Ngaoundéré, Douala, and Yaoundé. Once educated, the women were placed in professions as nurses or teachers. See Chantal Ndami, "La dynamique de la participation des femmes à la vie politique: le cas du Parlement camerounais, 1960-1997," MA Thesis, Université de Yaoundé-I, 1997, 16-17.

[17] From *La Voix du Cameroun*, No. 9. Aug-Sep 1952, as quoted in Joseph, "Birth," 218.

[18] ESOCAM organized on 20 June 1949 in the Sanaga-Maritime under the leadership of Bassa notables, including Pierre Dimalia, a former member of the UPC. Its political objective was to support the French project of integrating Cameroon into the French Union. French administrators assisted ESOCAM in the formation of anti-UPC committees throughout the Sanaga-Maritime, the UPC stronghold. ESOCAM soon faded out and was replaced by a predominately Bassa *Coordination des Indépendants Camerounais* (INDECAM) formed at Edea in 1952. Joseph, 176-77. Um Nyobé described ESOCAM as an organization "that upholds colonialism for little bribes." Ruben Um Nyobé, *Ecrits sous maquis*, Paris, 1989, 48-9.

assimilation politics. ESOCAM's petitions to the UN mentioned women only in situations that had direct relevance for men. For example, in 1949, the same year the *comité féminin de l'UPC* petitioned the UN for the first time, ESOCAM advocated greater "domestic education" for women, "as experience has shown us that [intellectually and culturally] educated women nearly always look forward to rising above African society," and Cameroonian women "are not sufficiently trained in household duties.[19] European education supposedly caused Cameroonian women to want to marry white men, and ESOCAM believed that for the sake of the country's well-being, the education of women should extend only to the domestic sphere.[20]

Although Cameroonian women actively participated in the UPC from its beginnings, the official formation of UDEFEC occurred in response to an international interest in the role of women in the party. UDEFEC attracted the interest of the Communist women's NGO, the Women's International Democratic Federation (WIDF), based in Berlin, which offered financial and moral support to the Cameroonian women's party.[21] The quickly growing WIDF inspired the UPC women to compose the statutes that led to the official organization of UDEFEC. In late 1951, WIDF

---

[19] Petition from the Evolution social camerounaise concerning the Cameroons under French administration, 22 Nov 1949, UNTC.T/PET.5/54.

[20] Ibid.

[21] WIDF formed in Paris in 1945 under the direction of Eugénie Cotton, a physicist and socio-political activist on an international scale. WIDF was a non-governmental organization with consultative status with the UN. Its stated objectives were "uprooting fascism and ensuring democracy in all countries; building a happy future for coming generations; giving women the rights contained in the International Women's Charter." See WIDF, *Eugénie Cotton*, Berlin [1970?].

correspondents with UPC members invited a female Cameroonian delegate to Vienna to discuss the planning of the International Conference in Defence of Children, held on 12-16 April 1952. Emma Ngom Mbem, accompanied by André Claude Nyobé, member of the Director Committee of the UPC, traveled to Vienna to represent Cameroonian women at the pre-conference meeting. [22] Marie-Irène Ngapeth-Biyong - Secretary General of UDEFEC at its inception - told how upon her return to Douala in February of 1952, Emma Ngom Mbem:

> *gathered all the women in Douala together. She gave us the summary account of her mission [to Vienna] and she spoke to us. Someone said something that interested us especially. Most of the associations at the conference had as part of their foundation associations that took care of children. And we had observed that in our territory, during the colonial period, Cameroonian children were not well taken care of. And we decided that very day that we too would form a women's organization to look after, not just children, but also the condition of women.* [23]

WDIF's international support served UDEFEC as the RDA and the PCF served the UPC, linking Cameroonian UPC and UDEFEC members with an expanding global struggle against imperialism. Urged on by the sense of belonging to an international movement for improving the status of all women, UDEFEC leaders provided the members they summoned with the knowledge that women worldwide shared many of their same concerns. An international NGO

---

[22] Interview with Marie-Irène Ngapeth-Biyong. It was after Ngom Mbem's return that UDEFEC formed in Douala.

[23] Interview with Marie-Irène Ngapeth-Biyong, Yaoundé, 6 July 1999.

with consultative status with the UN, the WIDF advocated peace and an end to fascism, focusing particularly on the rights of women and children.

Furthermore, the WIDF supported "the actions of women in all colonial and dependent countries for an end to their ghastly poverty and against colonial oppression;" and "all movements for national independence and for the protection of the sovereignty of all nations." [24] With these goals in mind, the WIDF strove to bring women together at international conferences, selecting a particular theme for each conference. [25] In February 1954 it published a pamphlet devoted to women in Africa entitled, *That They May Live; African Women Arise.* [26] The pamphlet revealed the economic exploitation of the colonies, the high rates of infant mortality, and labor abuses and gave a brief summary of the various women's anti-colonial protests in Kenya, Nigeria, the Gold Coast, Nyasaland, Senegal, The Sudan, Madagascar, the Cameroons, Morocco, Algeria, Tunisia, and Egypt. After the French administration banned the UPC, JDC, USCC, and UDEFEC in July 1955, the WIDF provided support to exiled

---

[24] Ibid.

[25] Their activities included an "International Commission to examine the conditions of Women Political Prisoners in Franco's Prisons" in 1948, a "Women's fact-finding Commission to the Countries of South-East Asia" in 1948, and the "Women's International Commission to investigate atrocities committed by the U.S. and Syngman Rhee troops in Korea." See WIDF, *The Rights of Women, Defence of Children, Peace,* Berlin, n.d. See also Report of the Women's International Commission for the Investigation of the Atrocities Committed by U.S. and Syngman Rhee Troops in Korea, Established by the WIDF," 19 June 1951, United Nations General Assembly, S/2203.

[26] WIDF, *That They May Live; African Women Arise*, Berlin, 1954.

members of UDEFEC in Nigeria, China, and Czechoslovakia.[27]

Whether or not every member of UDEFEC could envision herself as part of an international movement advocating human rights for all, each member had a sense of the movement extending beyond her own locale. The conception of women from afar supporting the nationalist cause of Cameroonian members was demonstrated by the popularly narrated account of UDEFEC's creation. Mrs. Menon, a representative of India in the General Assembly's Fourth Committee in 1953, was remembered in UDEFEC oral history for having prodded Ruben Um Nyobé to encourage Cameroonian women to organize politically. At local meetings throughout Babimbi from 1955 to 1957, the head of the regional delegation, Marianne Nsoga, told the women gathered at UDEFEC meetings that UN representatives asked Um Nyobé whether there were any women in Cameroon. Um Nyobé immediately sent a telegram to UPC leaders in Douala and asked them to organize a women's wing. Thus UDEFEC was created.[28] This story is one of several told at local meetings concerning the origins of UDEFEC. Although it is inaccurate - UDEFEC had formed at least eighteen months before Mrs. Menon's inquiries - it underscores the ideological significance of international women advocating on Cameroonian women's behalf. At the same time, this story of origin emphasizes Um

---

[27] Interview with Ngapeth-Biyong. On the activities of *upécistes* in exile, see Meredith Terretta, "Nationalists Go Global: From Forest *Maquis* to a Pan-African Accra," *Journal of African History* 51.2 (2010): 189-212.

[28] See, for example, Réunion d'UDEFEC, 7 Dec 1956, and La Grande Conference d'UDEFEC, Section de Babimbi, 4 Dec 1956, 1 AC71, ANY; and Report of the Trusteeship Council, 5 Dec 1953, Fourth Committee, 393rd Meeting, UNGA, 8th Session, Official Records, A/C.4/SR.393.

Nyobé as father of the larger nationalist movement of which UDEFEC was a part over the role of the women in founding UDEFEC.

The Relationship between the UPC and UDEFEC

The autonomous nature of UDEFEC has been deemphasized in the historiography, but was the cause of much debate as the party was formed. UDEFEC members recognized Um Nyobé's authority as spokesman for all three wings of the nationalist movement, and spoke of the UPC as "both mother and father" of UDEFEC. Nevertheless, the leaders of UDEFEC presented the UPC message in ways that spoke for the concerns of their women members, and UDEFEC maintained control of its organization and finances. Like the UPC, UDEFEC was organized in a pyramid structure, from local committees, to regional committees, with a director's committee at the top. At local meetings, delegates were elected to travel to scheduled regional meetings, or general congresses. The mobility of UDEFEC members combined with the pyramid structure of locally organized meetings enabled the party to survive even after it was officially dissolved. By 1956, the party had gained popularity and taken root among women, joining the increasingly radical fight against colonialism following the French administration's official ban of the nationalist movement in May 1955. UDEFEC's role had developed so significantly that Um Nyobé was compelled to send out a memo defining its purpose and position vis-à-vis the UPC.[29]

---

[29] Um Nyobé, Union des Populations du Cameroun, Section Kamerunaise du Rassemblement Démocratique Africain, Bureau du Comité Directeur sous maquis, "Relations entre l'UPC et l'UDEFEC dans la lutte pour

He explained that women could best address nationalistic issues that dealt with maternity, markets, public water pumps, and other activities outside male domains. Um Nyobé clearly expressed the UPC's official support of UDEFEC: "The UPC approves of UDEFEC's action. If UDEFEC only struggled for the interests of women, the UPC would be glad, because the UPC wants freedom and a better life for every Cameroonian, man or woman." [30] He urged the two companion movements to join together in the collaborative fight: "If UDEFEC fights for the liberation of Kamerun, the UPC rejoices." [31] He dissuaded women from acting as "separatists" by joining UDEFEC and refusing membership with the UPC, and likewise cautioned men not to force their wives to join the UPC and withhold their membership in UDEFEC. He promised that those who attempted to control UDEFEC or JDC activities would face disciplinary sanction from the UPC, comparing them to the repressive colonial administrators:

> *If UPC comrades have intents of taking charge of UDEFEC or the youth movement, it means that they have appropriated the language and assertions of colonialists who claim that UDEFEC and the JDC are mere affiliates of the UPC and do not represent separate movements.* [32]

Conclusion

UDEFEC's formation points to three characteristics of the popular nationalist movement in the entanglement of

---

l'indépendance du Kamerun," 30 September 1956, as quoted in Marie-Irène Ngapeth-Biyong, *UDEFEC*, 2-10.

[30] Ibid., 7.

[31] Ibid.

[32] Ibid., 8.

43

post-war Cameroonian politics. First, the UPC's active promotion and support of UDEFEC indicated its commitment to a democracy that included women's political participation. By contrast, ESOCAM's refusal to recognize women as political actors was consistent with its elitist, opportunistic objectives - to uphold the privileges of a few elite *évolués* by cooperating with the French administration, while barring political access to the population at large. ESOCAM's political platform confined women to the domestic sphere.

Secondly, UPC and UDEFEC ideology combined with post-war international concern over human rights to shape a Cameroonian worldview that stigmatized colonialism as racist and unjust – a violation of the ideals outlined in the Universal Declaration of Human Rights created at the UN in 1948. Capitalizing on Cameroon's trusteeship status that theoretically promised the UN's protection, the UPC and UDEFEC accepted international support from anti-imperialist allies. Not only did these leftist international allies provide financial and legal support to the UPC and UDEFEC; they also instilled their members with a consciousness of other colonized peoples' struggles throughout the world. [33] Um Nyobé and the leaders of UDEFEC who traveled abroad returned home to transmit the enthusiasm and optimism created in this new age of

---

[33] Although the French administration portrayed the party as communist, thus giving the French MRP government cause to suppress it, the party's ideology was less consistent with global communism than it was with anti-imperialism. Insofar as imperialism in Cameroon was represented by the British and French administrations, the party was essentially anti-colonial, and with its tendency to support every man or woman in his or her own pursuits, was more populist than communist in nature.

human rights and transregional anti-imperialism to as many Cameroonians - men and women - as possible.

Finally, UDEFEC responded to Cameroonian women's desire to organize. Although the French administration dismissed UDEFEC as no more than a UPC strategy to increase its number of supporters, UDEFEC founders had been seeking to establish a women's association since before 1952. The UPC's *Comité féminin* had expressed women's concerns to the Trusteeship Council in 1949. Marie-Irène Ngapeth and Marthe Ouandié briefly served as officers in the *Union des femmes camerounaises* (UFC) (a companion movement to ESOCAM).[34] In 1953 Julienne Niat complained to the French administration and had them expelled for becoming members of UDEFEC and carrying out "Communist activities" while still a part of the UFC.[35] Despite their differences, the women of both parties perceived the rights of

---

[34] The date of the UFC party's foundation is unclear. To avoid confusion with UDEFEC, the party changed its name to *Association des femmes camerounaises* in 1953. Ndami cites P. Nchamukong Bih, "The Evolution of Cameroonian Women in Politics," MA Thesis, Université de Yaounde I, 1990, 81 as writing that the *Association des femmes camerounaises* was formed by Laurence Dieng Maladi in 1946 with women's suffrage as its primary goal. However, both women and men *évolués* were accorded the right to vote in 1946 in French Cameroun. In 1952, mothers of at least two children were given the right to vote. See Ndami, 32. The only women's organization formed before 1952 found in the present day archival records in Yaoundé was *Association des femmes de l'Union Française au Cameroun*, formed in Douala on 17 Sept 1949. See 2/AC 5604, ANY. It is not clear whether Bih was referring to this latter association, or the UFC under the name it took in 1953.

[35] Mme Félix Ngoumou, née Julienne Niat, to Haut-Commissaire de la République Française au Cameroun, 12 Jan 1953, 3 AC 3520, ANY. Ngapeth-Biyong explained in an interview that she and Ouandié left the UFC because of Niat's refusal to allow them to read the petition to be submitted in UFC's name to the 1952 UN Visiting Mission.

women to be closely linked to democracy. Niat wrote to Governor Soudacaux in 1953:

> *The committee considers that there can be no democracy or full liberty in a country where women do not enjoy equal rights in society and are kept apart from political and cultural life.*[36]

Although the two parties both promoted women's rights and believed the participation of women in government to be a necessary step to take in Cameroon's transition to democracy, their paths would diverge drastically in a few short years as the political landscape became more fragmented. Niat, after a failed attempt to be elected to the Territorial Assembly of Cameroun in 1953, redoubled her efforts in 1956 and, although defeated in the assembly, headed the list of the Autochthonous and Allochthonous Peoples of the Wouri, demonstrating her popularity with the Douala electorate.[37] In 1956, Mrs. Ngapeth-Biyong would be hiding out on islands in the Wouri estuary with her four small children stowed away at her mother's house in Douala and her husband hospitalized for a bullet wound in the leg.[38] How could these two women with the common purpose of bringing Cameroonian women into politics arrive at such dramatically opposed positions in just three years? Chapter 3 will explore the political agenda of UDEFEC, attempting to explain how the movement became so subversive as to incur extreme repression by the French administration.

---

[36] Ibid.

[37] Ndami, 25. Ndami suggests that Niat's increase in popularity demonstrated by her greater success in the second election resulted from her having married between 1953 and 1956.

[38] Interview with Ngapeth-Biyong.

Chapter 3

UDEFEC's Political Awakening

The women of UDEFEC organized in 1952, but would not officially approve the party statutes until the first UDEFEC Congress in August 1954.[39] Beginning in 1952, UDEFEC focused on rights of women and children as well as issues of social and economic concern such as steep fees for selling goods at market, the unjust appropriation of land by the French administration, inadequate medical and educational institutions, and racial discrimination in the cities. Nevertheless members and leaders of UDEFEC only gradually began to perceive these issues as political as the French administration stepped up its repression of UPC nationalism. After Um Nyobé's efforts to lobby the General Assembly in 1952 and 1953, he returned to Cameroon and spoke publicly about the importance of women's visibility in politics.

Little by little, UDEFEC members recognized that no other Cameroonian political party supported their claims the way the UPC did, and as a result they soon realized the importance of entering the political arena. UDEFEC women began to understand the political significance of petitioning the UN as they assumed the role of speaking for the people and in so doing, creating a counter-narrative to the French administration's annual reports to the UN. From Babimbi to the Bamileke region, the women of UDEFEC wrote to set the record straight, exposing the failure of the French

---

[39] UDEFEC, *Union démocratique des femmes camerounaises*, Douala, 1992?, 15. See pp. 20-25 for a complete list of its 26 statutes.

administration to serve the Cameroonian peoples' best interests. In Babimbi, the women of UDEFEC demonstrated the pernicious effects of the administration's neglect of infrastructure. They described the decrepit ferry that served as the only way to cross the Sanaga river that separated the economic center of Douala from Babimbi as a cause of fatal accidents. In the Bamileke and Mungo regions, women of UDEFEC protested the administration's appointment of chiefs who sought personal gain at the financial and social detriment of their people.

In 1954 and 1955, the UPC increased its popular visibility by regularly organizing regional congresses that attracted growing numbers of members. Um Nyobé traveled tirelessly, speaking at UPC, JDC and UDEFEC gatherings. The party created unifying symbols that were easily diffused, such as a national anthem and a national flag. More importantly, the UPC distributed copies of Um Nyobé's speeches to the General Assembly in tracts and party newspapers, making UPC political strategies readily accessible to members. Traveling delegations carried this information with them, and at UDEFEC meetings, leaders read aloud Um Nyobé's speeches, the Universal Declaration of Human Rights, and the UN Charter. They related the origins of UDEFEC and its purpose in ways that were easy to understand, even for those women in rural areas, lacking urban experience. They invented songs and enacted skits to ensure the transmission of the UPC message in a way that was both memorable and entertaining.

UDEFEC grew in numbers and in organization throughout its first two years but only presented the Visiting

Mission with one petition in November of 1952.[40] Drawing on issues raised at the International Conference in Defence of the Child held in Vienna in 1952, the petition contained a localized list of WIDF principles. The petition described the unsuitable conditions of maternity wards, a lack of nutrition, unfit living quarters, deficient educational institutions, and the need for child labor laws.[41] Although conservative in tone when compared to later UDEFEC petitions, the document already contained the signature references to UPC principles. In its closing paragraph, the petition attributed the social misery it decried to the improper application of the Trusteeship system, and demanded immediate reunification and a fixed date for independence.

UDEFEC did not become prominent in Trusteeship Council records until 1954, the year after Um Nyobé's second visit to the UN to speak before the Fourth Committee of the General Assembly in December 1953.[42] Um Nyobé returned

---

[40] Interview with Ngapeth-Biyong who said: "On ne faisait pas la politique à l'époque." UDEFEC, Pétition remise à la Mission d'enquête du Conseil de Tutelle de l'ONU en visite au Cameroun, 1 Nov 1952, Douala. This petition does not appear in the Trusteeship Council records.

[41] Ibid.

[42] The members of the Trusteeship Council challenged Um Nyobé's presentation of the UPC as the political party with the greatest amount of popular support since UPC candidates not been elected to the Territorial Assembly. Um Nyobé explained that when elections had been held for the second electoral college - the college of indigenous inhabitants - the results had been challenged in ten out of 19 districts, and declared void in 3 districts. The administration, fearing a UPC victory, was reluctant to hold elections again. Um Nyobé also described the political tension in the territory, citing attempts on his life at Foumban, the military and police force's disruption of UPC meetings, and the confiscation of published tracts at customs. These various forms of harassment thwarted the UPC's political success, although he had photographs of the crowds in attendance at public meetings to prove the movement's popular success.

to publicize the discussions, holding public meetings throughout Cameroon in 1954, as he had after speaking before the Fourth Committee in December 1952.[43] Turning to petitions as a way for the population to express their support for the party despite the rigged elections, Um Nyobé encouraged the preparation, circulation, and collection of petitions to the UN.[44] He inspired UDEFEC women to begin petitioning at the first UDEFEC Congress in August 1954. Ngapeth-Biyong said of UDEFEC's first Congress:

> *This is where we began to make nationalist demands. ... We too began to send petitions to the UN to support the nationalist demands made by the UPC in 1954.*[45]

Politicization of UDEFEC in the Sanaga-Maritime and the Bamileke Regions

Although the women of UDEFEC did not define their purpose as explicitly political until late 1954, Um Nyobé already benefited from widespread popular loyalty, particularly in the Sanaga-Maritime. One of the reasons he achieved such popularity was that his supporters did not view him solely as a politician. For most inhabitants of the region, involvement in politics implied complicity with the foreign administrators, whereas Um Nyobé's claims carried an

---

United Nations General Assembly (hereafter UNGA), 8th Session, 4th Committee, 393rd Meeting, 5 Dec 1953, A/C.4/SR.393.

[43] Um Nyobé speaking to the 4th Committee, ibid.

[44] See Richard A. Joseph, *Radical Nationalism in Cameroun: Social Origins of the UPC Rebellion*, Oxford: Clarendon Press, 1977, 231: "In the absence of an 'open' electoral system, the UPC's only alternative to the ballot was the petition."

[45] Interview with Ngapeth-Biyong.

implicit entitlement to Cameroonian land and wealth for Cameroonians. Certainly he had nothing in common with opportunistic civil servants, chiefs appointed by the administration, or the elitist *évolués* seeking political advancement by declaring their support for the French Union. Instead, he was *Mpodol* – "he who speaks in the name of the people."[46] In other words, his supporters in the villages of the Sanaga-Maritime perceived him as too close to themselves to be a politician. He was their son, the one who would lead them to independence – the freedom from the humiliating burden of colonialism.[47] Their commitment to Um Nyobé politicized the people of the Sanaga-Maritime as, following his lead, they appropriated for themselves the fight against French rule.

As the administration's attacks on Um Nyobé became widely known, the people rallied to his defense and in so doing, awakened to the idea that a political sphere could exist outside an arena dominated by French administrators. When members of the nationalist movement and its sympathizers understood that Um Nyobé's goal was to eradicate French political influence altogether - they began to realize the importance of their own political role. This galvanized a popular rejection of colonialism in the collective imaginary,[48]

[46] Achille Mbembe, "Pouvoir des morts et langage des vivants: Les errances de la mémoire nationaliste au Cameroun," in Jean-François Bayart, et al. eds., *Le politique par le bas: Contributions a une problématique de la démocratie*, Paris, 1992, chaps. 5 and 6, explains the cultural significance of this term in the Sanaga-Maritime.

[47] Ibid., 195-196.

[48] Achille Mbembe, "Domaines de la nuit et autorité onirique dans les maquis du Sud-Cameroun (1955-1958)," *Journal of African History* 31.1 (1991): 93. For Mbembe, the revolution in Africa must take place first and foremost in the imaginary. In other words, major political change occurs through a restructuring of a collective vision. Um Nyobé's distance from

and this rejection was soon made manifest in the behavior of UPC and UDEFEC members.

In the Sanaga-Maritime, women's transition to politics was illustrated by their use of the act of petitioning. In 1954, the UPC's traveling delegations educated women to the importance of expressing their support of Um Nyobé through petitions to the UN, making them conscious of the ideological battle being waged. Two petitions from Eseka in 1953 and 1954 illustrate Cameroonian women's realization that they needed to participate in political discussions lest they be spoken for or their silence be mistaken for complicity with the administration. On 19 February 1954, the Women's Association of Eseka wrote to deny their authorship of an anti-UPC letter received by the UN on 25 November 1953.[49] In October 1953, the Chief Sub-Divisional Officer of Eseka had visited the Women's Association Chairman, Rosalie Menyim, and asked her to draft a letter "in the name of our association denouncing Um Nyobé, refuting and insulting him as she pleased."[50] Menyim returned home and asked a scribe to draft a letter stating "that our association had nothing to do with politics."[51] When she brought the letter to the office, the Chief Sub-Divisional Officer's interpreter, Paul Biyaga, told her that the letter did not contain what she had been ordered to write. He typed another letter, and took it in to the Chief Sub-Division Officer who sent him back to

---

the politics of the French administration and its corrupt supporters made Cameroonian independence possible in the imaginations of his supporters.

[49] Petition from the Association of the Women of Eseka concerning the Cameroons under French Administration, 19 Feb 1954, T/PET.5/254, UNTC.

[50] Ibid.

[51] Ibid.

hand-write it and to force Menyim to sign it. The illiterate Menyim told the Chief Sub-Divisional Officer "that she had never been able to read and write and that she could therefore not sign a letter for which she did not know the origin."[52] Not to be deterred, the Chief Sub-Divisional Officer instructed Menyim to hold the back of his hand while he signed the letter in her name. The Women's Association were told of the "shocking" contents of the letter "only when a certain petitioner, already in the territory, made his reporting tour."[53] The women of Eseka declared that they had never "sent any petition to oppose the hearing of Mr. Um Nyobé whom the Cameroonian people fully trust," and that such a letter was nothing but "the administration's machinations."[54]

Babimbi had for several years been an anti-administration political hotbed. Some 70 km outside of Douala, in the heart of the Sanaga-Maritime, Babimbi stagnated economically in comparison to the regions east and west of them.[55] In an attempt to shake off this stagnation, Pierre Penda had formed *Solidarité Babimbi* (SOLIBABI), a planters' cooperative. SOLIBABI members discussed the economic status of their

---

[52] T/PET.5/254.

[53] Ibid.

[54] Ibid. This petition was signed by Rosalie Menyim and ten other women, with each name bearing a fingerprint next to it.

[55] The Sanaga-Maritime region produced only small amounts of cocoa and coffee, and although the major agricultural crops were palm oil and palm nuts, these were not marketed, much less exported. The French administration drew on the region for manual laborers, spurring large numbers of migrants to Douala or labor sites such as ALUCAM (the aluminum producing plant in Edea). The subsequent decrease in population led to greater economic stagnation, and administrators were reluctant to construct the badly needed roads and bridges that would have permitted the Babimbi population to get their goods to market. See Joseph, *Radical Nationalism*, 111-14 and 136-39.

region, and focused on the difficulty of carrying agricultural produce to markets in Edea. Disliked by the Chief Sub-Divisional Officer, Xavier Béliard, for his "xenophobia" and insubordination towards French administrators, Penda was arrested on 21 April 1953 and imprisoned without trial. He was accused, among other things, of linking SOLIBABI to the UPC, and using the cooperative's funds to support Um Nyobé's trips to the UN General Assembly in New York. The UPC took up Penda's cause, collecting funds to hire a defense attorney from France to represent him.[56] In so doing, the UPC awakened the Babimbi population to the political issues of arbitrary arrest and imprisonment without trial, insisting that these transgressions violated Penda's human rights and as well as the UN Charter and Trusteeship Agreement.

On 24 September 1954, a ferry capsized on the Sanaga river while crossing from Songmbengu to Sakbayeme and caused the loss of some 50 lives. A petition with over 400 signatures reached the UN days later, sent by the "Babimbi People" and criticizing the lack of infrastructure that had led to accidents on the Sanaga in 1952, 1948, and 1936. The lack of roads, hospitals, and schools pointed to the government's negligence and misuse of the people's taxes: "The people of Babimbi want Article 76 of the UN Charter applied" read the petition.[57] The petitions about the ferry accident demonstrated the continuity between Penda's efforts to improve Babimbi's infrastructure and the UPC's understanding of the human rights norms defined in UN

---

[56] See Achille Mbembe, *La naissance du maquis dans le Sud-Cameroun. 1920-1960*, Paris, 1996, 238-243.

[57] Petition from the Babimbi People Concerning the Cameroons under French Administration, 29 Sep 1954, T/PET.5/322.

documents as petitioners argued that the lack of development constituted a violation of their human rights.

The UDEFEC leaders in Douala took up Penda's cause the year after his imprisonment. A petition signed by the directors of UDEFEC, Emma Mbem, Marie-Irène Ngapeth, Marthe Ouandié, and Marie Meïdo, protested against "the imprisonment and deportation of Pierre Penda, a member of the association SOLIBABI, for his efforts to ameliorate the infrastructure and living conditions by shedding light on their sad state."[58] The women referred to Penda as "a martyr of the indigenous population's struggle for social and economic progress and for liberty." In UDEFEC's characteristic emphasis on the rupture of family ties, they noted that Penda was deported to the jail at Yoko, in the North of Cameroon "just when his wife and three children were expecting his return home."[59]

Two months later, Marthe Penda, writing as the Secretary of the Babimbi branch of UDEFEC sent a petition on behalf of the "women of Babimbi, members of UDEFEC, the only women's organization in the Cameroons fighting alongside men to raise their own standard of living and that of the population." [60] Her petition also denounced the lack of infrastructure from a woman's perspective. She described the lack of care for pregnant and birthing mothers, the lack of orphanages, insufficient education that prompted youths to "drift to the big cities," and the lack of provisions for widows. Referring to the people of Babimbi as "our children," she cited the inability of farmers to cross the river

---

[58] Petition from the office of UDEFEC concerning the Cameroons under French administration, 1 Oct 1954, UNTC, T/PET.5/365.
[59] Ibid.
[60] Petition from the Babimbi branch of UDEFEC, 13 Dec 1954, UNTC, T/PET.5/409.

with their harvests as a cause of poverty. She requested the construction of a Kpongo - Ngambé - Bafia road that would facilitate travel to Douala. Marthe Penda referred to the Universal Declaration of Human Rights' fifth anniversary, "to draw the Secretary-General's attention to the fact that the Administering Authority is failing to observe the Declaration."[61] Serving as intermediary between the UN and Babimbi, the UDEFEC directors' committee, based in Douala, built a bridge between international human rights and local politics.

In late 1954, after the Visiting Mission's tour, many women began to express their resentment of the administration's attempted censorship and disruption of their meetings.[62] In November, the Trusteeship Council received several petitions from UDEFEC complaining that armed forces had broken up their peaceful meetings and confiscated their petitions for the Visiting Mission, "during an unlawful search of the UPC office on the pretext that Cameroonian women had no right to submit petitions to the UN."[63] The administration's attempt to silence UDEFEC members increased their determination to address the UN directly.[64]

---

[61] Ibid.

[62] Petition from Miss Annette Eleanore Biyaga, Douala, 10 Nov 1954, UNTC, T/PET.5/368.

[63] Petition from Mme. Martha Ngo Mayag, 12 Nov 1954, UNTC, T/PET.5/502. See also Petition from Miss Annette Eleanore Biyaga, Douala, 10 Nov 1954, UNTC, T/PET.5/368: "Our written petitions, signed by 48 women, were seized by the authorities at the Bureau of the UPC."

[64] This struggle for the right to petition is consistent with Joseph's theory that the French administration's early hostility to the UPC party pushed its members, and UDEFEC's into increasingly radical opposition. See Richard Joseph, "Nationalism in Postwar Cameroon: The Difficult Birth of the UPC," *Journal of African Studies* 2.2 (1975): 201-29, 228-29.

Politicization of UDEFEC in the Bamileke and Mungo Regions

In the Bamileke region, the UDEFEC branch at Fonkouakem began to protest against French intervention in local politics. They protested the "French tyranny in our Territory," spreading "dismay and panic throughout our country."[65] Two French officials had supported the takeover of Mbafam village by Mbonda Elie, appointing him "chief over the people against our wishes."[66] The people of Mbafam organized a delegation to march on the Sub-Divisional office to express their disapproval to the Chief Sub-Divisional Officer after having informed the French authorities in advance of their peaceful protest. The French sent in troops from Mbanga, Nkongsamba, Bafoussam, and Bangangte who joined with the forces of pro-French Kamga Joseph, the traditional chief of Bandjoun, to block the delegation. Members of UDEFEC who participated in the march described the violent reaction they faced as they approached the Sub-Divisional Office:

> *Hardly had the delegation arrived when its members were set upon by the troops. We were confronted with a terrible and tragic scene: blows and injuries, mass arrests followed by imprisonment. And we returned home, sorrowful and dismayed.*[67]

Bamileke opposition to the administration had developed after Chief Djoumessi of Dschang began to distribute coffee

---

[65] Petition from the UDEFEC Branch of Fonkouakem, 22 Nov 1954, UNTC, T/PET.5/512.

[66] Ibid.

[67] Ibid.

seeds to the population at large, and to pay his farm laborers in wages. [68] First through *Kumsze*, [69] and then as the first President of the UPC, Chief Djoumessi, organized an initiative for Bamileke chiefs to stand up to the French administration in local economic and political matters. This initiative involved an attempt to economically empower Bamileke planters by liberalizing the distribution of coffee seeds (a lucrative cash crop in the region) and by increasing wages for Bamileke laborers. Those chiefs who continued to collaborate with the French administration by confining the distribution of coffee seeds to a select group of approved planters or over-taxing their people began to be perceived as exploiters seeking their own personal gain. Like Um Nyobé in the Sanaga-Maritime, Djoumessi and the traditional chiefs who supported him orchestrated a radical break with the French administration, rendering its outright rejection thinkable on a large scale. Like Um Nyobé, Djoumessi defined a political terrain outside the administration's control. Thereafter, the administration's attempts to appoint or depose Bamileke chiefs ignited popular resistance. The

---

[68] Ndobegang M. Mbapndah, "French Colonial Agricultural Policy, African Chiefs, and Coffee Growing in the Cameroun Grassfields, 1920-1960," *The International Journal of African Historical Studies* 27 (1994): 41-58, 57. Although the French policy since the 1920s had been to allow only a handful of elites to have their own coffee plantations, Djoumessi advocated the participation of all Africans in the coffee economy. He was also the first chief in the Bamileke region to pay his workers after the abolition of forced labor. He paid higher wages than the European plantation owners, and was resented by the latter as well as some Bamileke chiefs. Those chiefs who supported Djoumessi's efforts joined him, first in *Kumsze*, the Traditional Association of Bamileke Peoples, and then by allying themselves with the UPC. When Djoumessi became the first president of the UPC, his popularity in the region most likely allowed the party to take root quickly.

[69] See chap. 2, above.

women of UDEFEC in the Bamileke region carried out this resistance, first by participating in the march on the Chief Sub-Divisional Office, and then by writing to the UN about the administration's violent repression of the peoples' peaceful demonstration.

By the end of 1954, Cameroonian women in the southern and western regions of French Cameroon had become active participants in nationalist politics. Adding their voices to their husbands', fathers' and brothers' in the UPC, they became accustomed to appealing to the international supervisory body of the UN to intervene in matters they perceived as unjust. It remained for the women's party to take root, spread throughout the regions, and gather members. The next year, the efforts of Roland Pré's administration to eradicate the nationalist movement would provide them with the impetus to do so.

The Creation of a Visible Popularity

In early 1955, the UPC, the JDC and UDEFEC reached the high watermark of their legal organization under the French administration. As their meetings drew larger and larger audiences, the administration subjected members and leaders to ever increasing harassment. UPC leaders wrote that beginning with the arrest of the UPC leaders elected at the 1950 UPC Congress at Dschang,

> *the meetings, even if authorised by the Government are regularly troubled and dispersed by the police or the army, any protest or strike is dealt with brutally, those taking part in them are disbanded and arrested.*[70]

---

[70] UPC Foreign Delegation, *The Kamerun,* Cairo, 1957, 30.

The administration monitored UPC participation in elections by controlling access to documents required to exercise voting privileges such as "identity cards, birth certificates, marriage certificates, census numbers."[71] After the General Assembly questioned Um Nyobé about the popularity of the UPC movement, Um Nyobé's strategy became to build popular support that would be visible in spite of the irregular elections. Threatened by the party's increasing visibility and growing numbers, the French administration countered by expanding its repressive strategies.[72]

After Roland Pré replaced André Soucadaux as High Commissioner at the end of 1954, the administration fostered the growth of community organizations, youth groups, and women's associations throughout the territory to increase its own influence and "make life impossible to the members of the UPC."[73] However, the UPC, UDEFEC, and the JDC had already put down roots throughout the territory that minimized popular support for these new organizations. Pré also moved the UPC leaders to Douala where he could supervise them more easily. But, wrote the UPC foreign delegation:

---

[71] Ibid., 29.

[72] E. Mortimer considered the "dominant facts of Cameroun politics between 1950 and 1955" to be "the growing strength of the UPC in organization and publicity and its failure to register this in terms of votes." See Edward Mortimer, *France and the Africans 1944-1960: A Political History*, London, 1969. Joseph suggests that the administration's effort to prevent the UPC from participating in the elections rendered the UPC a greater threat to stability. See Joseph, *Radical Nationalism*, 183.

[73] UPC, *The Kamerun*, 31. From late 1955, UPC, UDEFEC, and JDC members employed the German spelling, "Kamerun," to indicate their desire for a unified territory. See Ruben Um Nyobé, *Problème national kamerunais*, Paris, 1984, 11.

to the great confusion of Mr. Pré, those upécistes who are set aside are usually replaced by others of the same kind, for want of a 'non-upéciste' staff. Since then a collective hysteria has possessed the minds of all European leaders in the Kamerun.[74]

Meanwhile, in Douala, rumors spread among party members that Pré had been granted permission to imprison Um Nyobé and that he promised to suppress the movement completely in less than six months.[75]

Driven to a sense of urgency by these rumors, the UPC, UDEFEC, and the JDC met with greater frequency throughout the territory, attracting larger numbers and becoming more and more organized. Beginning in 1954, UPC, UDEFEC, the JDC, and USCC meetings promoted a growing sense of solidarity, even as they awakened political thinking territory-wide. The desire for freedom from foreign economic dominance, racial discrimination, land appropriation by the Department of Water and Forests, and meddling in local politics were all framed as the UPC's demand for independence and reunification.

In carrying Um Nyobé's message to the people, the nationalist movement carved out a new strategy of popular expression and a widespread the transmission of information. Leaders read letters, tracts, petitions to the UN, and meeting minutes aloud to local meetings, familiarizing all members with the party's internationalist strategy. The parties began to publish periodical newspapers, including, *L'étoile*, *Lumière*, *Le*

---

[74] Ibid., 33.

[75] Ibid. and Petition from Mme Gertrude Omog in the *maquis*, 14 June 1955, UNTC, T/PET.5/674, and Joseph, *Radical Nationalism*, 243-46. Pré's lack of response to letters sent by the UPC indicating Um Nyobé's willingness to discuss a compromise lent credibility to these rumors.

crabe noir, *La voix du Cameroun*, and UDEFEC's *Femmes Kamerunaises*.[76] The administration often confiscated these publications, in an attempt to prevent their distribution.[77] Members gathered to discuss the making of party policy in public meetings, and relied on these diverse venues to keep them informed. Members also contributed to the body of information about the party, by writing, or by speaking at public meetings. The exchange of information flowed both ways, not just from the leadership to the membership at large.[78]

The movements relied heavily on oral expression such as songs, speeches, sayings, visual images and symbols, and skits to convey the message.[79] The most essential of these included the UPC national anthem, the national flag, and the Joint Proclamation publicly announcing the solidarity of UPC, UDEFEC, JDC, and USCC members. Not only were the songs easy to remember, they encouraged a collective participation from members, and were compatible with the party's commitment to making its platform widely accessible. The UPC had popularized a national anthem at its inception in Douala in 1947, and members began every meeting,

---

[76] *Femmes Kamerunaises* was the official mouth-piece of UDEFEC, edited by Marthe Moumié, but neither Mbembe nor Joseph mention it in their lists of the progressive party's published political ephemera. Marthe Moumié also wrote for other papers, for example, "La discrimination raciale a l'égard de la femme camerounaise," *Lumière*, Feb 1955, 3.

[77] UPC, *The Kamerun*, 30. In December 1953, Um Nyobé told the UN's 4th Committee that French authorities had seized 10, 000 copies of the text of the statement he made before the General Assembly in 1952, which the UPC had published as a tract entitled *Ce que veut le people Camerounais*. UNGA, 8th Session, 4th Committee, 393rd Meeting, 5 Dec 1953.

[78] This distinguished the UPC from political parties such as ESOCAM that tended to impose their strategies and policies from above.

[79] Interview with Ngapeth-Biyong.

whether a small base committee meeting or a mass gathering, by singing the anthem.

On 22 April 1955, the UPC, UDEFEC, the JDC, and USCC issued a "Joint Proclamation of the Trusteeship system for the establishment of a sovereign Cameroonian state," which demanded immediate independence for the territory.[80] The Proclamation contained three specific requests:

1. General elections to be held before 1 December 1955 for the purpose of setting up a constituent National Assembly.

2. An Executive Board to be established immediately in the form of a Provisional Government responsible for the organization of the general election.

3. A United Nations Commission to be set up immediately in the Territory to supervise the installation of the organs of the new Cameroonian State.[81]

By unveiling the Joint Proclamation before crowds in Douala and Yaoundé, the nationalist movement demonstrated their increasing solidarity and numbers publicly. UDEFEC printed a copy of the Joint Proclamation in their newspaper, *Femmes Kamerunaises*, which officially marked their undeniable involvement in politics.

An essential popular symbol was the official flag of the UPC, unveiled as the Cameroonian national flag before some

---

[80] The Joint Proclamation marked Um Nyobé's switch from the demand for the UN to fix a date for independence to the UPC leaders' selection of 1 December 1955 as the date. See Mbembe, *Naissance*, 328 and Ruben Um Nyobé, *Ecrits sous maquis*, Paris, 1989, 100.

[81] Joint Proclamation for the Termination of the Trusteeship system for the Establishment of a Sovereign Cameroonian State, 22 April 1955, T/PET.5/612. The UDEFEC members' signatures included Marthe Moumié, Gertrude Omog, Lydie Matip, Marthe Bahida, and a delegation from the North.

1, 500 people in Yaoundé on 22 May 1955. A black crab on a red background, the crowd was told that the flag symbolized the achievement of independence in the hearts of the Cameroonian people.[82] The black crab symbolized a united Cameroon by referring to the unified territory's name, after the Rio dos Cameroes, or the river of shrimp, and the crab's black color denoted an anti-colonial solidarity other black Africans struggling for their independence. The red background symbolized the blood spilt for the nationalist cause.[83] Even before unveiling their own flag, the UPC had popularized the UN flag as a symbol of their struggle for liberation and as a reminder that Cameroon was not a colony, but a trusteeship, and thus looked to the UN to liberate its people from an unjust colonialism.[84]

The flag, the national anthem, and the Joint Proclamation symbolized a popular unity that in turn attracted more people to the movement, promoting UPC visibility, and bestowing a collective sense of pride in identification with the nationalist project. At the meetings, signing on to petitions addressed to the UN Visiting Mission became another unifying ritual. By May 1955, UDEFEC members had added their voices to those of UPC nationalists, entering the political dialogue in local areas and within the international sphere at the UN.

---

[82] Mbembe, *Naissance*, 328 and Um Nyobé, *Ecrits*, 100. The same flag is used to represent the UPC and UDEFEC today.

[83] Um Nyobé, *Ecrits*, 100-03.

[84] UPC, *The Kamerun*, 33.

Chapter 4

The Official Ban of the Nationalist Movement, And Reorganization in the *Maquis*

Who can count the victims of the Sanaga-Maritime and all of Kamerun:
the dead, the prisoners, the refugees in foreign lands, the freedom fighters?
How many huts burned, hamlets partly or totally set ablaze? Plundered
goods, plundered and stolen and destroyed, cattle stolen and slaughtered?
Who can count the bereaved, the widows and the orphans?
How can one soothe the women of Sanaga-Maritime or elsewhere,
the women whose husbands are dead somewhere, or in prison, or fighting
in the maquis, or who knows where [...]?

– *Reverend Pastor Abomo Akoa's Easter sermon, 1957*[1]

The French administration's official ban of the UPC on 13 July 1955 came at the height of the party's popularity. As a result, the proscription pushed the party into uncharted waters of heightened anti-colonial militancy as nationalists denounced it as a violation of the UN Charter and the French Constitution. UDEFEC leaders found themselves listed side by side with UPC men on the administration's warrants for arrest. If UDEFEC had formed primarily as a women's social organization, it now had little choice but to join the full-fledged fight - in ideology and in practice - against the administration. The official ban on the party disrupted the very things UDEFEC had formed to protect - family stability and the social well-being of women and children. UDEFEC

---

[1] As quoted in UPC, *The UPC Denounces the Planned Systematic Tortures in the Kamerun,* Cairo, 1958, 57-8.

members began to view the administration as more than an institution that stood in the way of Cameroonian social and economic progress. Nationalists now framed the French administration as an active opponent waging a war against the nationalists and their families. UDEFEC leaders were quick to define the arrests and punishments following the party's ban as a human rights crisis. The French administration's use of arrest and imprisonment separated many UPC members from their wives, which in turn prompted more women to turn to UDEFEC and the UPC for support and to demand justice. The conversion of members' homes to meeting places for the UPC and UDEFEC after the administration's ban on the movement's public meetings led troops under French control to conduct intrusive searches in private homes.

The Official Ban of the Nationalist Movement

The French administration, under the direction of Roland Pré, spent the first months of 1955 setting in motion events that it could use to justify the official ban of the nationalist movement on 13 July 1955. On 19 February 1955, Pré authorized all judicial and civil authorities "to summon the army to scatter any meeting of the progressive movements."[2] The French administration viewed UDEFEC as part of UPC strategy to increase its membership and to discourage the French administration's use of force during mass gatherings:

> *The UDEFEC was born of the desire to associate women with the active work of the party, the women being called upon to take*

---

[2] Ibid., 30, 33. This decree applied to "suspicious meetings of more than two persons."

part in demonstrations so as to paralyze the police action by their presence.[3]

Not to be deterred by the presence of women in the demonstrations, the administration threatened and arrested men and women activists alike.

On 19 and 25 April 1955, the police conducted an illegal search at UPC headquarters and leaders' homes. They arrested 24 active members including Theodore Mayi Matip, the president of the JDC,[4] Jacques Ngom, the leader of the USCC, Ruben Um Nyobé's wife, and Gertrude Omog, a member of UDEFEC from Edea.[5] Um Nyobé's "infant child was snatched from its mother's arms and handed over to the welfare authorities."[6] Matip was deported to the Mokolo fortress, a "hell-like prison" in Maroua, with many other nationalist party members including Martha Bahida, a member of UDEFEC who was pregnant at the time. Bahida gave birth in the Mokolo prison.[7] UPC and UDEFEC petitions emphasized that the arbitrary arrests and conditions

---

[3] Observations of the French Government as Administering Authority, 6 Dec 1955, UNTC, T/OBS.5/71.

[4] Theodore Mayi Matip would be, in 1958, the only UPC nationalist to know the exact whereabouts of Ruben Um Nyobé and his family in the *maquis*. He became Um Nyobé's trusted diviner and dream interpreter. Some believe that Mayi Matip revealed Um Nyobé's hideout to the administration's troops that assassinated him. See Achille Mbembe, *La naissance du maquis dans le Sud-Cameroun, 1920-1960*, Paris, 1996, chap. 12.

[5] Petition from Mme Gertrude Omog in the *maquis*, 14 June 1955, UNTC, T/PET.5/674; UPC Foreign Delegation, *The Kamerun*, Cairo, 1957, 31, and interview with Henriette Ekwe, Douala, 16 June 1999.

[6] Petition from Mme Gertrude Omog in the *maquis*, 14 June 1955, UNTC, T/PET.5/674.

[7] UPC, *Tortures*, 16, 42. For a petition sent later, describing the inhumane conditions in the northern prisons, see Petition from Political Prisoners in Yoko Penitentiary Concerning the Cameroons under French Administration, 6 Nov 1958, T/PET.5/L.463.

of imprisonment constituted human rights violations. UDEFEC members underscored the particular hardships that imprisonment imposed on pregnant women or nursing mothers.

In Douala, on May 13th, police arrested 73 nationalists, of whom 37 were women. About forty civilians were injured.[8] In a petition to the UN, women of UDEFEC would later describe this day:

> *The Cameroonian people of Douala assembled in a crowd before the Law Court to support its best-loved leaders, and harsh repressive measures were taken against them, resulting in 40 wounded, of whom one woman, Liga Tecla, had to spend more than three weeks in hospital, and 70 persons arrested, 37 of them women, among whom seven were breast-feeding babies under one year of age.[9]*

The 37 women measured their common cell - 3 by 2.5 meters - with a meter-long head-scarf. The women kept their spirits up in the prison by singing "for a long time to reaffirm their ardent desire to see the Cameroons achieve its Unification and Independence" and were doused with naphthalene for their enthusiasm.[10]

Just days after the flag ceremony in Yaounde on 22 May 1955,[11] riots erupted in Douala, Yaoundé, Nkongsamba, Bafoussam, and Babimbi, across the country from the southern Sanaga-Maritime to the Bamileke region.[12] UPC

---

[8] UPC, *The Kamerun*, 31.
[9] Petition from UDEFEC and the UPC concerning the Cameroons under French administration, 19 June 1955, T/PET.5/717.
[10] Ibid.
[11] See chap. 3 above.
[12] Um Nyobé's plan was for the Cameroonian people to achieve independence without bloodshed. For two detailed accounts of the

nationalists in exile wrote later that the French administration had instigated the riots because they had "ambushed" the UPC by sending a delegation from Houphouët-Boigny's RDA to infiltrate their meetings in 1955. [13] Houphouët-Boigny had split from the French Communist Party (FCP), and affiliated his branch of the RDA with Mitterand's *Union Démocratique et Sociale de la Résistance* in 1952. [14] The French administration used the UPC's refusal to distance itself from the FCP to portray nationalists as dangerous and threatening to global democracy, in order to justify its suppression of the party. As nationalists attempted to expel the infiltrators from meetings, violence erupted and the police and military stood ready to intervene and arrest UPC, UDEFEC and JDC members. The May riots precipitated what *upécistes* would call the "Reign of Terror" during which French administrators in Cameroon brought troops from French West Africa to "drown the progressive movements in blood." [15]

On 28 May 1955, eight hundred warrants were signed and "distributed in all the regions to facilitate the arrest of all

---

cumulative provocation of the French administration's deputies and gendarmes, see Mbembe, *Naissance*, chap. 10, and Richard A. Joseph, *Radical Nationalism in Cameroun: Social Origins of the UPC Rebellion*, Oxford: Clarendon Press, 1977, chaps. 8 and 9.

[13] In 1957, the UPC foreign delegation in Cairo insisted that the riots were provoked by the Administration's "ambush" on the UPC - that is, the administration's attempt to push the UPC towards compromise, following Houphouët-Boigny's RDA break with the FCP. UPC Foreign Delegation, *The Kamerun,* Cairo, 1957, 34. See Joseph, *Radical Nationalism* 181-3 for an account of the RDA sections' split. Among the sections opposing Houphouët-Boigny's decision to break with the FCP were the UPC and RDA sections in Niger and Senegal.

[14] Mortimer, 173.

[15] UPC, *The Kamerun,* 35. For an account from an UDEFEC petitioner, see the fifteen-page missive sent by Mme Gertrude Omog in the *maquis,* 14 June 1955, UNTC, T/PET.5/674.

members of the progressive movements." [16] Hundreds of those listed were jailed or deported. On 13 July 1955, shortly before the arrival of the UN Visiting Mission, the French Council of Ministers issued a decree dissolving the UPC, the JDC and UDEFEC. The administration's legal basis for the proscription was a law issued on 10 January 1936 in Algeria that permitted the suppression of private militias seeking to establish their own government through force.[17] All leaders and members of the UPC who had not been persecuted during the May "riots" were arrested or forced into exile "on the charge of reconstitution of a dissolved association, for having mentioned the UPC or national objectives."[18]

The list of party leaders marked for arrest included women leaders of UDEFEC such as Marie-Irène Ngapeth and Gertrude Omog. Many of those from the Douala area escaped to the islands in the Wouri estuary, where they hid out in conditions that were particularly adverse for women with small children. Marie-Irene Ngapeth wrote that after the initial riots on 25 May in Douala:

---

[16] UPC, *The Kamerun,* 35. See also UPC, *Tortures,* 12-13.

[17] Ibid., 35. See also Circular from Roland Pré, Le Haut Commissaire de la République Française au Cameroun to Messieurs les Chefs de Région, 25 July 1955, 1 AC 1969, ANY. The UPC submitted arguments to the *Conseil d'Etat* and to the UN that the July 1955 ban was invalid since it applied only to French colonies, and therefore not to a Trusteeship Territory, and that the UPC was not an armed militia. The ban heightened the stakes of conflict between the UPC and the administration, and would not be repealed until 1960 by the independent Cameroun government (and then only temporarily). See Joseph, *Radical Nationalism,* 317.

[18] UPC, *The Kamerun,* 36. Um Nyobé split ways with Félix Moumié, Ernest Ouandié, Job Ngapeth, and Abel Kingue, over the use of violence to achieve their goals. Um Nyobé went south to Sanaga-Maritime. and the others regrouped at Kumba. See Ruben Um Nyobé, *Ecrits sous maquis,* Paris, 1989, 200-03, and Mbembe, *Naissance,* chap. 10. especially 327-340.

during the day of 27 May there were raids and tortures in the same quarters, and summary trials followed by convictions and deportation... the sole victims of which were members of the progressive movements. Next came an exodus to the bush and to the forests, with the most tragic consequences; mothers dragged along their very young children or abandoned them like orphans in their huts; no-one knows how many people died, from hunger or eaten by wild beasts.[19]

Marie-Irène Ngapeth spent three months in the Wouri with her four youngest children. The children suffered from malaria, and Ngapeth feared for their health. She managed to have them carried back to her mother's house in Douala, where, according to her husband, they lived "in dire poverty, closely watched by the French police, who are ready to arrest anyone attempting to take care of them on suspicion of being in touch with us."[20] Like many of the UPC, JDC and UDEFEC members who went underground, Ngapeth eventually left the Wouri and escaped to Kumba, in the British Cameroons, where she and other leaders reorganized a UPC headquarters in exile.

The WIDF manifested its continued support of UDEFEC after the proscription in a petition to the Trusteeship Council denouncing the "serious cases of repression in the Cameroons."[21] Quoting from UDEFEC petitions, WIDF urged the UN "to bring the repression to an end, to give the women and children of the Cameroons a

---

[19] Petition from Marie-Irène Ngapeth, Kumba, 20 June 1955, T/PET.5/913.

[20] Petition from Jean-René Ngapeth Chubah, Notable of Badiangsen, Subdivision of Bangangté, 14 Aug 1955, UNTC, T/PET.5/916.

[21] Petition from Angiola Minella, General-Secretary of WIDF, 14 Oct 1955, Berlin, UNTC, T/PET.5/818.

chance to live in peace, and to ensure the respect for the rights of a people under Trusteeship."[22] Furthermore, WIDF insisted that the dissolution of UDEFEC prevented "Cameroonian women from expressing their aspirations and claiming their own and their children's rights."[23]

As UDEFEC was forced underground, the members continued writing, increasing their international visibility and appealing to an international sense of justice. Back home, they continued to organize, and the movement grew -- in the *maquis*.

UDEFEC in the *Maquis*: Babimbi

After the forced dissolution of the nationalist liberation movement, UDEFEC members devoted their political energies to internationally protesting the violence unleashed against them and their comrades. They rapidly built clandestine links between regions, relying on the pyramidal structure of the movement, which permitted local committees to maintain contact via the traveling regional committee leaders who went from meeting to meeting.[24]

The volume of petitions flooding the Trusteeship Council described a Cameroon very different from the one Roland Pré wanted to portray for the up-coming Visiting Mission, scheduled for November of 1955. The administration began to monitor the mail and confiscated all UPC, UDEFEC, and

---

[22] Ibid.

[23] Ibid.

[24] Likewise, the UPC began relying on the regional sections as intermediaries between the Central Committees and the Executive Committee after July 1955, and before than the Central Committees -- grouping at least five base committees -- had been linked directly to the Executive Committee. Joseph, *Radical Nationalism*, 229.

JDC correspondence, particularly from prisoners.[25] A JDC member described the process of sending petitions from the *maquis* after the French ban of the parties:

After the French government had dissolved the progressive movements in 1955, petitions and cables to the UN were held up and the petitioners who tried to send them were prosecuted. Since then petitioners living in the Eastern zone of the Territory have been obliged to come and send their petitions from the Western zone. As troops are posted all along the frontiers, the only way the petitioners can go is through the bush and they sometimes take more than ten days to reach the western zone. In order to reduce travelling expenses and save time, the active members of a committee or a branch collect all their petitions and cables and delegate two or three of their comrades to go and send them off from the Western zone under British administration.[26]

Messengers caught with UPC petitions outside the post office were arrested, but could escape if they had enough cash to bribe the police, usually out of UPC funds for postage.

The leaders of UDEFEC were conscious of petitioning's importance as a political tool and understood that the UN disapproved of the administration's censorship of inhabitants' political expression within the trust territories. Gertrude Omog, wrote from the *maquis* to emphasize the correlation between freedom of expression and political freedom:

---

[25] UPC members complained from prison of their correspondence being censored and interrupted altogether, making it impossible for them to contact lawyers. UPC, "Detention," 30 July 1955, 1 AC 1977.

[26] Petition from the Merged Branches of the JDC Concerning the Cameroons under British Administration, 2 Aug 1957, T/PET.4/144/Add.l.

They [the French authorities] will institute proceedings against anyone who writes to the UN to state the facts [about the May 1955 riots], and French judges will be found to issue warrants for the arrest of such persons, including myself, on the grounds of giving false information and of defamation. Who will verify the proceedings in a regime where some people are always right and others are always wrong? That is why we have said and written, and continue to say and to write, that only in an independent Cameroon shall we be able to enjoy freedom, because to write or cable the UN is to threaten the security of the French state, the geographic boundaries of which extend as far as Douala, and to inform the UN of concrete facts is to fall foul of the law and to deserve the scaffold.[27]

The petitions from the leaders of UDEFEC after the official ban reacted against a regime that broke current protocols of the international rule of law and transgressed France's own constitution. Mrs. Omog's words identified her with a larger cause – that of appealing for Cameroonians' political and civil liberties within the greater international context of human rights and international relations:

As a Cameroonian citizen and a woman who believes in the ideal of the UN, namely the strengthening of international peace and security, I am sending you this petition and ask that you have it considered by the next General Assembly. ...

During the recent disturbances, women, even pregnant, were killed and imprisoned without reason merely because they were black,

---

[27] Petition from Mme Gertrude Omog, in the *maquis*, 14 June 1955, UNTC, T/PET.5/674. Omog's petition and others' contained up to date news reports from French newspapers that criticized Pré's oppressive rule, suggesting that the *maquisards* had connections with the outside world. Omog asked the Trusteeship Council to respond to her petition via an address in Paris as it was not safe to give her home address.

for I am convinced - and there are many examples to support my contention - that if they had been European women, more care would have been taken and the judges would have been more objective and sympathetic.[28]

Omog deliberately used language that she hoped would elicit a reaction among international human rights advocates involved in discussions about racism, gender-based discrimination, social and political justice and anti-imperialism.[29]

Mrs. Ngapeth spoke of a movement for independence, reunification and nationalism that grew in strength and influence after its official proscription:

The French government thought that in dissolving us, we would be eradicated just like that. But instead, we quickly organized. We began the clandestine fight in which UDEFEC militants played a significant role.[30]

The petitions from the of UDEFEC leaders indicated an awareness of the international situation, the legal workings of the UN Charter, the Cameroon territories' jurisdictional status as Trust Territories, and anti-colonial colonial struggles

---

[28] Petition from Mme Gertrude Omog, member of UDEFEC, *maquis*, 14 June 1955, T/PET.5/674.

[29] During the same period, petitions were being sent to the UN from African-Americans, the most notorious of which depicted racism against blacks in the U.S. as genocide. See Charles H. Martin, "Internationalizing 'The American Dilemma': The Civil Rights Congress and the 1951 Genocide Petition to the United Nations," *Journal of American Ethnic History* 16.4 (1997): 35-61, for an account of George Patterson and the Civil Rights Congress composition of We Charge Genocide, a petition sent to the UN in 1951.

[30] Interview with Marie-Irène Ngapeth-Biyong.

in other parts of the world. The leaders used precise French legal terminology, quoted from French newspapers, and referred to the Universal Declaration of Human Rights to appeal to an emerging definition in the West of human rights as universal. At the same time, the leaders understood that for it to thrive underground, the movement had to spread into the rural areas where the UN and notions of universal human rights were reinterpreted locally as they took root.

The surviving records from Babimbi - a stronghold of UPC, JDC, and UDEFEC resistance in the Sanaga-Maritime - describe the procedures that allowed local women to petition and to increase their involvement in the movement.[31] By the beginning of 1955, the stage had been set for Babimbi to become one of the centers of resistance against Pré's repressive measures. The links had been made, through the Penda affair,[32] between Babimbi and UPC leaders in Douala, and through the notoriety of the Penda case, the region's inhabitants had learned firsthand of the administration's "evil policy of arrest and imprisonment, repression, seizures, persecution, and slander."[33] Babimbi provided the ideal center for UDEFEC to reorganize and increase in numbers after the ban of the movement in July 1955.

In late 1955 and throughout 1956, UDEFEC women risked the administration's "ambushes" to attend local committee meetings held in members' houses. After the official ban of UPC, UDEFEC and JDC parties, members held meetings in their homes since private dwellings were

---

[31] The Babimbi UDEFEC records are contained in the file 1AC 71, ANY. Many of the meetings were recorded in Bassa, although the majority were recorded in French.
[32] See chap. 3, above.
[33] Ibid.

protected under French penal code.[34] However the police and military did not hesitate to intrude into homes to break up meetings, to conduct searches, to confiscate documents, and to arrest any suspected members. Thus the administration's violence against nationalists shifted from the public meetings spaces – markets, town squares, and public halls – to the intimate spaces of private homes.

Meetings usually began with a rendition of the "Kamerunian" national anthem, and a recapitulation of the movement's history. Often a member of the traveling regional or sectional delegation would read from recent UPC tracts, thus transmitting the most recent strategies of the party to all members, whether literate or not. After the reading of the tracts, the member presiding over the meeting would impose a fifteen-minute reflective silence. One of the meeting's leaders usually spoke about Um Nyobé as the liberator of the nation, and credited him with sparking the development of UDEFEC. For example, at a meeting in the Babimbi region in December 1956, Ernestine Mouthamal explained that a UN representative had asked Um Nyobé whether women participated in the fight for independence. He answered that they needed to, and sent a telegram back asking that the Cameroonian women organize meetings for themselves.[35]

In some cases the president of the meeting would tell stories containing illustrative proverbs. At the Conference of

---

[34] Liberté de réunion, 30 June 1881, modified 28 March 1907. Public meetings could be forbidden by municipal or administrative decision if they posed a serious threat to public order. Meetings on private property with an individually invited audience were free. See Lambézat à toutes régions sauf Douala, Edea, Nkongsamba, Yaoundé, 11 Mar 1953, 1AC367, ANY.
[35] Réunion d'UDEFEC, 7 Dec 1956.

the Babimbi Section held in the home of Emilienne Bayiha on 4 December 1956, Marianne Nsoga told the story of the prodigal son to illustrate how ESOCAM did not plan for the nation's future.[36] In many cases, UDEFEC members drew parallels with the Israelites' search for the Promised Land, describing Um Nyobé as their Moses, the prophet who would liberate them by the grace of God. Nsoga advised members at Kikot to turn to their Bibles for strength.[37]

UDEFEC members kept surprisingly meticulous records, considering their outlawed status, but Um Nyobé had emphasized the importance of record-keeping to demonstrate the movement's popularity to the UN.[38] In September 1956, the UPC section at Babimbi sent out an UDEFEC delegation under the direction of Mariane Nsoga with specific orders to keep record of her tour throughout the region and of the results of the elected regional and sectional committees.[39] Nsoga instructed local and regional committees to keep a notebook within which to systematically record meeting minutes and the names of those attending. The meeting secretary logged the name of each woman in attendance, along with the name of her village, her occupation, and her age. Depending on the location of the meetings, the occupations included housekeepers, seamstresses, farmers, and teachers. The meetings were attended by women ranging

[36] La grande Conférence d'UDEFEC tenue par la délégation de la Section de Babimbi assistée dans la maison du Camarade Bayiha Emilienne, 4 Dec 1956,1 AC 71, ANY.

[37] Réunion du 6 Nov 1956 tenue au domicile de la camarade Bibulu Marie sur la proposition de la délégation au comité local, Kikot II.

[38] See Introduction and chap. 2, above. This meticulous record-keeping has continued in the Bassa region as one of the many residual effects of the nationalist movement in this area.

[39] UPC, Section Kamerunaise du RDA, Section de Babimbi, Mandat 13 Sep 1956, 1 AC 71, ANY.

in ages from ten to very old, although in the Pendjock regional section, most women in attendance were in their 30s and 40s. Ngapeth-Biyong remembered that there were some very old women in UDEFEC:

> *Yes, there were even old women. They spoke Pidgin English, you know.... They were very, very dynamic. Illiterate, but they had discussions, and brought up political issues. We made it up as we went along: How women should construct a point of view, how to express ourselves.*[40]

If no literate women were present, as in the case of the meeting held in the home of Emilienne Bayiha on 4 Dec 1956, a secretary – in this case, Jacques Bayiha – recorded the meeting minutes.[41] The issue of literacy posed the greatest problem in the North. None of the UDEFEC members in Garoua could read or write, nor did they use French. They relied on men to translate and write out their petitions to the UN.[42] At least one literate member was essential to every local meeting. In this time of political struggle that relied on the ability to write to the UN, the necessity for literacy overrode gender boundaries in local meetings. In rare cases, the literate member was a woman, in a meeting dominated by men.[43]

---

[40] Interview with Ngapeth-Biyong.

[41] La grande conférence d'UDEFEC, Section de Babimbi, 4 Dec 1956, 1 AC 71, ANY.

[42] Interview with Ngapeth-Biyong.

[43] Such was the case, evidently in the Petition from Mrs. Tecla Azan and 8 others, Yaoundé, 2 Nov 1959., T/PET.5/L.494. In some locales, where UDEFEC meetings did not exist, women held positions in local UPC committees.

Meetings were used to collect membership fees and funds used to send petitions and telegrams to the UN, for leaders' and members' travel, and after 1955, for the purchase and importation of weapons to prepare for the armed fight against the French and those who the movement's leaders viewed as their collaborators. In 1956, a membership card cost 100 CFA francs, subscription cost 250 CFA francs and a membership of ten was required to make an official local committee. Each local committee member was to help to create others and when a meeting grew to 25 or more members, it was divided into two meetings. When UDEFEC members traveled to attend a regional meeting, or a congress, the local committee funded the trip to the meeting place, and the hosting party funded the trip home. The visits of the regional delegation to the local committees provided a sense of regional solidarity and strength. The visiting delegation in Babimbi, headed by Marianne Nsoga, encouraged local committees by underscoring their essential value for the movement. At Billangue, Nsoga told members:

> *It gives me great satisfaction to see so many of you. It shows us that Kamerun, the land of our birth, will have its final victory. You are like teachers coaching small children; your duty is to teach the masses that our only purpose is to ask for immediate independence and reunification for our country.*[44]

In another meeting, Nsoga told members that the purpose of UDEFEC was to give voice to the claims of women, to send petitions to the UN, and to demonstrate and protest against the abuses of the colonial regime. She told the

---

[44] Regional committee meeting, UDEFEC, Babimbi, 2 October 1956, 1 AC 7I, ANY.

local leaders that they were like catechists, sent to teach the masses and she entreated them to "join together to fight against the colonialists who plunder the fruits of our soil."[45]

Following the precedent established by UDEFEC's response to the unjust imprisonment of Pierre Penda, petitions poured into the UN from women in the Sanaga-Maritime telling stories of their husbands' cruel and life-threatening imprisonment after the movements had gone underground. Because male prisoners could not rely on the mail system, the responsibility of exposing the conditions of the prisons and the irregular judiciary proceedings faced by members of the UPC often fell to women.[46] Martine Ngo Bata's husband, Francois Tembten, was arrested and detained in a cell at Babimbi. Martine Ngo Bata contended that:

because of Mr. Roland Pré's harsh and repressive treatment of prisoners, my husband was badly beaten by soldiers and received only two macabos and two spoonfuls of salt a day for food.[47]

---

[45] Renouvellement d'un nouveau Comité Local Kikot II, Réunion du 6 Nov 1956 tenue au domicile de Bihulu Marie sur la proposition de la delegation au Comité Local II, 1 AC 71, ANY. French Protestant and Catholic missions trained indigenous catechists, and sent them out to live in remote areas, where they served as educators - religious and scholastic. See Jean Criaud, *La geste des Spiritains: Histoire de l'Eglise au Cameroun,* 1916-1990, Yaoundé, 1990.

[46] Some UPC prisoners did manage to send detailed descriptions of the conditions of the prisons to the UN. The mass arrests following the ban of the movement led to overcrowding in the prisons. On 22 Aug 1955, the Chef de région of Nyong-et-Sanaga wrote to the *Procureur-Général* that the Yaoundé prison, designed to hold 300 inmates, now held 655. He suggested transferring them to prisons at Nanga Eboko, Akonolinga, and Mbalmayo (all towns in the same region). The Procureur-General's response was to build a new prison. See 1 AC 1977. ANY.

[47] Petition to the Chairman and members of the UN Visiting Mission to the Cameroons, Babimbi, no date, (registered at the UN on 4 Nov 1955), UNTC, T/PET.5/888, Section 11.

When she attempted to send food to the prison for her husband, the Chief Subdivisional Officer ordered two guards to whip her. Her husband fell ill in June and died on 19 September 1955 but she was not allowed to see his body.[48] Her petition, although not listed as coming from UDEFEC or the UPC, ended with the signatory call for the "immediate unification and independence of the people."[49] When the French Observatory Committee investigated the claims, Martine Ngo Bata told local authorities that a villager member of the UPC had written the petition, but she refused to divulge his name.[50] Her protection of the petitioner suggested that her loyalties were with the UPC.

Although UPC, UDEFEC, and JDC members were forced into the *maquis*, the movement had, by this time, taken root in the minds and hearts of the population of the Sanaga-Maritime. Ironically, the administration's repressive measures prompted the peoples' dependence on UPC and UDEFEC meetings, especially for those families who lost their husbands to the cause. Rebecca Ngo Nyoth, whose husband had fled to the *maquis*, wrote: "We are able to eat only through the help of the Mongue UPC Local Committee and we have nothing for clothes."[51]

While Sanaga-Maritime nationalists learned to live in the *maquis*, the rest of the UPC, UDEFEC, and JDC leadership attempted to reorganize the movement at Kumba. Straddling the border between the British and French Cameroons,

---

[48] Ibid., Section 12. See chap. 5 for the cultural significance of incomplete burials and unresolved deaths.

[49] Ibid., Section 11.

[50] T/OBS.5/94.

[51] Petition from Rebecca Ngo Nyoth, Dressmaker at Bipundi, *Maquis*, 13 July 1956, T/PET.5/919.

Kumba was centrally located to Douala, Victoria (a coastal town within the British territory), and Nkongsamba (a town in the Mungo, with a significant Bamileke population). Kumba provided an ideal headquarters for the UPC delegation in exile from the French territory to rebuild and to extend its influence into the Bamileke region and the British Cameroons.

UDEFEC in Kumba and the Bamileke region

After the leaders of the UPC, JDC and UDEFEC reorganized at Kumba, Emma Mbem, the president of UDEFEC, sent a telegram from Nigeria requesting a hearing for UDEFEC at the UN with Ngapeth as their delegate.[52] The leaders of the party prepared a "national educational conference" from 21 to 23 February 1956 to minimize factionalization in this new underground phase. Two days later, Marthe Moumié told the UN about the national educational conference and protested against the UN's refusal to hear the Cameroonian "democratic organizations."[53] She emphasized that the UPC, UDEFEC and JDC delegation at Kumba represented Cameroonians from both the British and the French territories.

Areas surrounding Kumba showed increasing UPC and UDEFEC organization after the movement was banned. In the Bamileke region, where the population was polarized between supporters of the UPC and those supporting the administration, the French administration increased its use of

---

[52] Telegram from Emma Mbem, Dec 1955, Lagos, Nigeria, UNTC, T/PET.5/L.75.

[53] Petition from Marthe Moumié, Adda Tjade, and Antoinette Biyong concerning the Cameroons under British and French administration, Kumba, 25 Feb 1956. UNTC, T/PET.4&5/L.10.

force to uphold the chiefs it deemed loyal.[54] At this time, the chiefs in the Bamileke region were choosing sides between the anti-colonialists such as Mathias Djoumessi, and the French administration. [55] Those chiefs who resisted the administration faced troops under French (and later the Cameroonian state's) control who terrorized their villages as well as the aerial bombardments. In many cases, nationalist chiefs were eventually forced to flee into exile to escape arrest and imprisonment. UPC leaders in exile purchased arms and smuggled them back into the Bamileke region for those who attempted to carry on the resistance. [56] Marcel Ngandjong Feze, who inherited the chieftaincy of Bandenkop in 1955 at age 18, ruled less than a year as a UPC supporter before French troops bombed his village and he fled to Accra,

---

[54] In 1954 the administration had encouraged the formation of MANJONG, *Parti-bamileke anti-upéciste.* MANJONG's platform consisted of little more than to oppose the UPC and reestablish its dominance in the Mungo: "We must join with the administration in order to make the UPC disappear. We will send a delegation to travel the Nkongsamba subdivision to teach moral ways to all Bamileke in order to eradicate the doctrine of the UPC in them." MANJONG referred to itself as an "Association des jeunes" while describing Kumzse as the "Association des vieux." This assessment of the anti-UPC traditional association being made up of juniors at odds with their elders runs counter to the existing historiography which lends to define UPC activists as the "social cadets" fighting against their elders. See Manjong, *Parti-Bamileke anti-upéciste*, 1955, 2 AC 31, ANY.

[55] On Djoumessi, see chap. 3.

[56] On arms smuggling, see Meredith Terretta, "Nationalists Go Global: From Forest *Maquis* to a Pan-African Accra," *Journal of African History* 51.2 (2010): 189-212. Ngapeth-Biyong told me that the women of UDEFEC smuggled weapons into the French Cameroon in the sacks of peanuts they carried to market. The women in Babimbi meetings were told that their membership fees would go towards the procurement of weapons. Interview with Ngapeth-Biyong.

Ghana.[57] According to Feze, only those chiefs who sought personal gains supported the administration and the chiefs instated by the French administration after the deposition of nationalist chiefs lacked popularity.

In August 1956, UDEFEC sent in petitions signed by thousands in the Bamileke region demanding the unification and independence of "Kamerun." UPC and UDEFEC petitioners in this region regularly protested French intervention in local politics and particularly when it came to the selection of traditional chiefs. Like in the Sanaga-Maritime, in the Bamileke region, the UPC and UDEFEC allowed local people to imagine a political terrain outside the structure of French or British dominance.

Conclusion

The women of UDEFEC had joined in the political struggles, public and clandestine, of their male comrades, intervening on their behalf, and expressing their own concerns. They had been punished by the violent rebuttals of the French regime, through the rupture of marriages and

---

[57] Interview with Marcel Ngandjong Feze, Chief of Badenkop, 15 July 1999, Bandenkop. Upon his departure, the French administration instated Feze's uncle as chief, although the people of Bandenkop contested their decision. Feze spent his years of exile in Ghana, where UPC leaders sent him to secondary school. After receiving his diploma, he received a scholarship from the Chinese government to continue his university studies there. He studied in China for eight years, received a masters degree, and learned to read, write and speak Mandarin, most likely at the University of Peking, Foreign Language School. Petition from Kamerunian Students in the Peoples' Republic of China, Peking, 7 June 1961, T/PET.4/L.177. He traveled back to Guinea-Conakry, spent 13 years working and settled with a family. In 1984, he responded to President Paul Biya's invitation for all those in exile to return to Cameroon. Feze was eventually reinstated as Chief at Bandenkop.

families due to imprisonment, death, or flight, and they had faced their own torture, incarceration, and forced exile. Once drawn into the fight, the leaders of UDEFEC demonstrated an acute awareness of their rights under the UN trusteeship system and within the larger context of human rights. They learned of other political struggles taking place between colonial powers and indigenous peoples elsewhere in the world. The UDEFEC leaders cultivated this political knowledge in the minds of their members, fulfilling their responsibility to educate. Members in local areas, in turn, diffused the movement's message - by writing on behalf of the imprisoned, opening their homes to meetings, and relying on petitioning as a channel through which to give voice to their own interpretations of the movement and its political purpose.

Chapter 5

From the City to the Village: The Rejection of the Colonial Curse

Le porteur de notre cou ... jettera la malédiction dans les eaux de la mer. / He who carries our neck will throw the curse into the waters of the sea.[58]

UDEFEC did not merely spread the political message of the UPC and protest the repression faced by the nationalist movements at the hands of the French and British administrations. UDEFEC's petitions clearly expressed socio-economic concerns and interests of the women they represented, drawing on the ideological foundations of the WIDF, and tailoring these principles to fit the specific needs of Cameroonian women. Furthermore, the party's socio-economic goals helped to forge a crucial link between urban and rural women. In both settings, women faced the economic discrimination that stemmed, not only from being colonial subjects under European administration, but also from belonging to the patriarchal order of Cameroonian society. Often these two forms of domination reinforced each other in the lives of women, and UDEFEC provided a forum within which members could denounce this pattern.

A divergence between women petitioners surfaced after the party went underground in 1955. The petitions from the

---

[58] Song from Kan, as quoted in Achille Mbembe, "Pouvoir des morts et langage des vivants: Les errances de la mémoire nationaliste au Cameroun," in Jean-François Bayart, et al. eds., *Le politique par le bas: Contributions a une problématique de la démocratie*, Paris, 1992, 196.

leaders indicated an awareness of the international situation, the legal workings of the UN Charter, the French constitution and penal code, and Cameroon's status, as well as colonial struggles in other parts of the world.

By contrast, the majority of petitions after 1955 originated from various regions throughout the territory, from the Sanaga-Maritime to the Bamileke region: those originating in more rural villages grouped into such subdivisions as Bafang, Nkongsamba, Bafoussam, Bangangte, Babimbi, Douala, and Wouri outnumbered those coming from the cities and towns. [59] As popular anti-colonial sentiment mounted, UDEFEC's narrative described the foreign administration as more and more threatening. From the international sphere, to the rural domestic and agricultural sphere, Cameroonian women came together under the auspices of a common purpose, identifying with one another as women attempting to ameliorate their own and their families' economic, cultural, and social lives. UDEFEC women throughout the territories constructed a nationalist narrative that underscored the importance of cultural education for their children, and sought to protect the economic interests of women merchants and agriculturalists. They called for the elimination of the cumbersome licensing systems for sellers in city markets, and rejected the administration's appropriation of their land through "scheduled forestry" policies in rural areas.

The women of UDEFEC began to see European bio-medicine, particularly in the realm of fertility and child-bearing, as endangering the health of Cameroonian women and society at large. Increasingly, they associated French and

---

[59] The petitions were sent in batches of up to sixty, usually mailed from Kumba in the British Cameroons, originating from towns and villages throughout the Bamileke, Sanaga-Maritime and Mungo regions.

British rule with a "perimeter of death,"[60] and believed that administrators had launched a strategy to exterminate members of the nationalist movement. By this point, their rejection of foreign administration was so complete that some petitioners actually wrote that they would prefer death to continued existence under the rule of the administering authorities. The women of UDEFEC enabled the large-scale rejection of foreign rule because they were present at nearly every juncture between the European administration and Cameroonians at large. Lifting their voices and their pens in UDEFEC, women in the cities and in rural areas were key in reclaiming the symbols of social well-being from colonial rule.[61]

From the Cities to the Village, the Women of UDEFEC Join Together

The city of Douala had provided fertile ground for UDEFEC since, in 1947, 71 percent of the female population were unmarried and most were salaried workers.[62] The anti-colonial message of the UPC and its companion labor union, the USCC, promised that independence would bring an end to the exploitation of workers and abolish strict licensing requirements for traders in the markets or self-employed tradesmen, such as taxi drivers or seamstresses. This message must have held an immediate appeal for single women, eking out a living in the city. As early as 1949, before the formation

---

[60] Achille Mbembe, *La naissance du maquis dans le Sud-Cameroun, 1920-1960*, Paris, 1996, 383-391 and Achille Mbembe, "Domaines de la nuit et autorité onirique dans les maquis du Sud-Cameroun (1955-1958)," *Journal of African History* 31.1 (1991): 89-121.
[61] See Mbembe, "Pouvoir."
[62] Mbembe, *Naissance*, 225-27.

of UDEFEC, the *comité féminin* of the UPC had requested the "abolition of licenses required for seamstresses working at home," and the freedom of women to sell alcoholic beverages and food provisions in public and private work yards, especially at meal times. [63] Mrs. Ngapeth-Biyong confirmed that the founders of UDEFEC in 1952 protested against the official fees for market stalls that French administrators required, because the party felt these fees unjustly targeted women sellers.[64]

As the administration's persecution of UPC and UDEFEC members increased in late 1954 and 1955, Roland Pré's administrators and police singled out members of the nationalist movement, subjecting city laborers and sellers to arbitrary searches under the pretense of verifying that they were licensed. The administration imprisoned them, confiscated their merchandise, or revoked their licenses on the slightest infraction. UPC and UDEFEC members found the bureaucracy particularly unmanageable when applying for licenses or identity cards, a process that forced them to wait abnormally long periods for any administrative paperwork. UDEFEC women claimed that these delay tactics constituted harassment and stifled economic activity in the cities.

In 1953, Mrs. Marie Mpaye wrote from Douala describing the burdens she and her husband faced as a result of French administrative policies and licensing systems.[65] Mrs. Mpaye's husband had been dismissed from the British firm R. W.

---

[63] Petition from the Comité féminin de l'UPC concerning the Cameroons under French and British administration, 20 Nov 1949, UNTC, T/PET.4/32.

[64] Interview with Ngapeth-Biyong.

[65] Petition from Mrs. Marie Louise Mpaye concerning the Cameroons under French administration, Douala, 29 Oct 1954, UNTC, T/PET.5/449.

King in January for forming a labor union for the firm's employees. He bought a car and got a public transport permit to work as a taxi driver. Shortly afterwards, "Mr. Ruben Um Nyobé hired this taxi and used it for his tours around our country to report his news from the UN,"[66] traveling to Foumban in March 1953 "at the time of the unfortunate events provoked by the colonialists of that area."[67] According to Mrs. Mpaye, the administration found her husband's "communist" and "anti-white" behavior so threatening that it impounded his taxi and issued "all sorts of instructions so that every one of his efforts to set up a business failed."[68] She and her family, including her elderly mother in Eseka, had been reduced to poverty as a result of the administration's discrimination against her husband for his support of the reunification and independence of Cameroon. Mrs. Mpaye requested the UN to intervene to restore her husband's transport permit or to arrange to have him receive unemployment. She ended her petition with UDEFECs socio-political message, insisting that "only the unity and independence of the Cameroons can guarantee the social life of the families of our country."[69]

UDEFEC leaders encouraged their members to think in terms of the association between political freedom and social and economic well-being. The party focused on the premise

---

[66] Ibid.

[67] Ibid. Um Nyobé told the General Assembly that attempts on his life had been carried out by supporters of the French administration. See UNGA, 8th Session. 4th Committee, 393rd Meeting, 5 Dec 1953, A/C.4/SR.393.

[68] Petition from Mrs. Marie Louise Mpaye concerning the Cameroons under French administration, Douala, 29 Oct 1954, UNTC, T/PET.5/449.

[69] Ibid.

that political injustice unleashed by the administration disrupted family life, both by limiting economic opportunities for Cameroonian nationalist entrepreneurs who refused to take handouts from the French administration and by tearing families apart by imprisoning and deporting the men. Members of the nationalist parties tended to view supporters of the administration as people who thought only of their own immediate financial gain, rather than looking ahead to the economic well-being of all Cameroonians.[70] In contrast, members of the UPC, the JDC and UDEFEC were fully aware that the benefits offered by the French administration were conditional and temporary.[71] UDEFEC members wrote in November of 1954 that "the colonial system, which has been plundering our country for forty years," was like "a hunter who throws rotting bananas in the tiger's path in order to wrest the game from his jaws."[72] Cameroonians who were complicit with European exploitation were seen as traitors to the rest of the population. The head of the traveling delegation in Babimbi, Marianne Nsoga, instructed local committee members to refrain from contact with colons and their "*valets*" - European administrators and businessmen, and their Cameroonian "lackeys."[73]

The leaders of the UPC and UDEFEC gained popularity with members in towns throughout the territory by protesting the payment of fees to the administration for the use of

---

[70] Interview with Marcel Ngandjong Feze. See also chap. 2, above.

[71] For example, Marianne Nsoga told a local meeting in Babimbi the parable of the prodigal son to illustrate how ESOCAM did not plan for the nation's future. See chap. 3, above.

[72] Petition from UDEFEC, Fonkouakem, Bafang region to the Chairman of the 4th Committee, 9th Session of the UNGA, 22 Nov 1954, UNTC, T/PET.5/512.

[73] Réunion d'UDEFEK à la maison de Mbok Souzanne, 6 Dec 1956.

market stalls. [74] In Yaoundé, Félix Moumié presided over meetings at which merchants met with *Confédération Générale du Travail* unionists to discuss the administration's restrictive economic policies. The discussion of economic subjugation surely galvanized members to attend the gathering of over fifteen hundred people on 22 May 1955 at which Moumié unveiled the Cameroonian "national flag" - the black crab on the red background. [75] Shortly thereafter, the editorial board of *Femmes camerounaises* wrote that "African women (especially Cameroonians)" felt the burden of colonial exploitation to be particularly heavy:

> *The social concept of colonialism lays strong stress on the inferiority of African to white women. Widows (sellers of foodstuffs) are often arrested in the markets for failure to pay the market fees ... Those poor women, who have no means of feeding their children, are thus wantonly penalized when they are forced to pay out all that they have earned during the day and remain empty-handed.* [76]

The women who signed the petition in *Femmes camerounaises* expressed the official UDEFEC view that market stall fees constituted gender and racial discrimination; and by 1955, it was apparent that the administration was using the licensing system to single out UPC and UDEFEC activists.

---

[74] According to Marie-Irène Ngapeth-Biyong, the protestation against market fees had been one of the leading causes taken up by UDEFEC's founders. Interview with Ngapeth-Biyong.

[75] See chap. 3.

[76] Petitions from the Editorial Board of the newspaper Femmes camerounaises concerning the Cameroons under French administration (signed by Marthe Moumié, Editor-in-Chief), 7 June 1955, UNTC, T/PET.5/618.

In April 1955, Anne Langue, a widow from Manjo in the Mungo region, described herself as a "dealer of goods and merchandise," an activity that provided the only source of income for her to support her six children.[77] On 26 March 1955, while she was at home looking after her children, her clerk, Nestor Noumba, went to market to sell her goods, forgetting the license for selling at her house. A police superintendent from Nkongsamba "arbitrarily impounded my goods and took them to Nkongsamba" and arrested Noumba.[78] Mrs. Langue asked the UN what citizenship means for Cameroonians, when the UN Charter and the Universal Declaration of Human Rights could be so violated. Noumba was an active member of the UPC, an alliance that certainly prompted his arrest.[79] The UPC denounced his arrest as one of the "simply provocative actions for the purpose of undermining the rights of a true Cameroonian people which seeks the Unification and Independence of this country."[80]

As members of the UDEFEC, the JDC and the UPC fled to British territory and reorganized the movement as One Kamerun, petitions came in from women complaining of the same restrictive and discriminatory licensing tactics employed by the British. Mrs. Theresia Nana, president of the women's committee of One Kamerun in Tiko wrote:

---

[77] Petition from Anne Langue, a dealer, mother of six children, widow of the late Leuton Augustin, former dealer, resident at Manjo station, Mungo region, 4 April 1955, T/PET.5/573.

[78] Ibid.

[79] Nestor Noumba would be killed by French troops in an ambush of the "*maquis de garde*" on 30 April 1958. He would later appear to Um Nyobé in a dream, pointing out a more secure hiding place in the *maquis*. See Achille Mbembe, "Domaines," 110, 113.

[80] Petition from Denis Nouenon, member of the UPC, 31 March 1955, T/PET.5/67.

At first women trade without buying license when the Administering Authority started to hunt women catching them as animals in the bush. [But] the Nigerian women are served with this license without delay.[81]

Women who attempted to sell goods from their houses in order to supplement their husbands' incomes were arrested for holding a "petty market at their doors."[82]

Economic matters linked UDEFEC members in the city with those in rural areas, particularly in the Bamileke, Mungo and Sanaga-Maritime regions, where women worked as the primary food crop producers for their families. In 1949, the *comité féminin's* first petition requested technological improvements for women farmers, including "the supply of agricultural machinery to free women from the toil of hoeing in plantations and of extracting palm oil by pounding."[83] The petition asked UN authorities to grant women the right to bear arms to protect their crops from marauding elephants and cattle.[84] The women also requested that the acquisition of

---

[81] Petition from Mrs. Theresia Nana, President of the Women's Committee of One Kamerun, Tiko, 5 Nov 1958, T/PET.4/156.

[82] Ibid.

[83] Petition from the Comité féminin de l'UPC concerning the Cameroons under French and British administration, 20 Nov 1949, UNTC, T/PET.4/32.

[84] See also Susan Diduk, "Women's Agricultural Production and Political Action in the Cameroon Grassfields," *Africa* 59 (1989): 338-55 and E. M. Chilver, "Women Cultivators, Cows and Cash Crops: Phyllis Kayberry's Women of the Grassfields Revisited," in P. Geschiere and P. Konings. eds., *Conference on the Political Economy of Cameroon - Historical Perspectives*, 1989, 383-421.

land by forestry companies be banned, except in cases in which the rightful owner of the land gave permission.[85]

Petitioners decried the French administration's appropriation of land under the scheduled forestry policy. The Fonkouakem UDEFEC committee wrote in 1954: "The foreigner makes use of this famous term to gain possession of our inheritance."[86] Administrative policy had evolved from "reserved forestry" classified by a decree on 12 July 1932, to "scheduled forestry" on 19 April 1948, which forbade the cultivation of lands that the French had set aside for their own use.[87] Information regarding the decree had not been made available to women farmers, and only after many of them had planted their crops had administrators attempted to retrieve the land. [88] The UDEFEC petition from Fonkouakem stated:

> *The colonialists have even found a 'scheduled forest' in an area of grasslands and crops with a dense population. That is what they call our plants, or the few trees which shelter us from the sun. Our*

[85] Petition from the Comité féminin de l'UPC concerning the Cameroons under French and British administration, 20 Nov 1949, UNTC, T/PET.4/32.

[86] Petition from UDEFEC, Fonkouakem, Bafang region, to the Chairman of the 4th Committee, 9th Session of the UNGA, 22 Nov 1954, UNTC, T/PET.5/512.

[87] Le Conservateur, Chef du Service des Eaux et Forets, à M. le Directeur des Affaires Politiques et Administratives, Yaoundé, 8 April 1954, 2 AC 1032, ANY.

[88] In 1955 the Service des Eaux et forêts was reorganized, thus the reinforcement of the decree could be related to this increased "efficiency." See 2 AC 1032, ANY.

arguments were not accepted and we were told that the forest had been scheduled before the land was cultivated.[89]

The petitions shed light on the ways that French policies affected the lives of women specifically. UDEFEC's strategic response to the burdens imposed by colonialism was to describe individual grievances, to turn those complaints into public knowledge, and to use them to reject foreign domination altogether.

Mrs. Lydia Dopo, a widowed planter near Loum in the Mungo region, protested scheduled forestry for years, by sending detailed correspondence both to French administrators in the territory and to the UN. Her husband had purchased land, for which she had a deed, in 1926. After his death in 1942, Mrs. Dopo inherited the land, which "included a plantation of cacao and coffee bushes, banana trees, and other fruit-bearing plants, and many other very valuable natural resources."[90] Mrs. Dopo had eight children to care for on the land she inherited. Around 1951:

The French Administration ... issued a Local or Ministerial Order placing all the forest in this area in the classified category, but it did so without first consulting the African planters who had occupied the land long before that decision was taken.[91]

---

[89] Petition from UDEFEC, Fonkouakem, Bafang region, to the Chairman of the 4th Committee, 9th Session of the UNGA, 22 Nov 1954, UNTC, T/PET.5/512.

[90] Petition from Mrs. Lydia Dopo, widow of the late Ndinang, planter at Boungue near Loum, 30 Nov 1954, UNTC. T/PET.5/400. Mrs. Dopo had written on four separate occasions, and included copies of the deed of land purchased by her husband in 1926 as well as a record of her inheritance in 1942.

[91] Ibid.

The amount classified as a forest reserve measured ten square kilometers. Mrs. Dopo linked her claims with the UPC's political platform, pointing out that French control of Cameroonians' land, "just when the Cameroonians aspire to national independence," constituted a violation of the UN Charter and set the Cameroons back in its advance towards independence. In a previous letter to the French High Commissioner, Mrs. Dopo gave a more detailed account of the administration's appropriation of her land:

> *On 12 February 1954, a European Official of the Water and Forestry Service asked me to go with him and show him the boundaries of my plantation... He stated that, if I did not go, the whole of my plantation would be classified as part of the private domain. He also added that I would have to bear the consequences of having written a letter. On reaching the plantation, he refused to accept the boundaries I showed him and I returned to my home. Remaining behind, he cut off a large part of my plantation, which was under cultivation, for classification in the private domain. From time to time this European official of the Water and Forestry service tells me that he will send me to prison [...] if I persist in claiming my rights. He has also asked me who wrote the letter I sent to you. I hope that the French Constitution, of which you are the guardian, guarantees freedom of expression to all citizens without distinction as to sex or social class.*[92]

---

[92] Lydia Dopo to the High Commissioner of the French Republic in the Cameroons, 28 Feb 1954, UNTC, T/PET.5/400. The French administration responded that Lydia Dopo had extended the boundaries of her plantation after 1948, the date of the decree designating the Territory's forest land, beyond the boundaries of the decree: "*Vous avez ainsi étendu vos cultures (cacaoyères, macabos, et arachides) en dehors des limites fixées en 1948 aux dépens du domaine privé du Territioire et à vos risques et perils.*" See M. Bouquet a Lydia Dopo, 5 Mar 1955, 2 AC 1032, ANY.

The French policy of scheduled forestry intruded directly into the lives of women agriculturalists attempting to provide for their families, just as the licensing requirements had targeted women sellers and seamstresses in urban areas. UDEFEC women thus resisted administrative control over women's lives in matters where they otherwise maintained a certain degree of autonomy.

Women in the Grassfields region seized the opportunity to challenge both colonial policy and the pattern of male domination of the cultivation of cash crops such as coffee. Beginning in the 1920s, increasing numbers of men from the Grassfields began to cultivate cash crops, such as bananas, cocoa, and after the Second World War, coffee.[93] The French had tried to control the amount of land allotted to entrepreneurs for coffee plantations in order to avoid famines. A decree of 4 July 1933 required that all coffee plantations be registered with the authorities and that new planters seek a permit from the sub-divisional officer. Those not allowed to grow coffee deeply resented this policy, viewing it as the administration's effort to control access to wealth. After the Second World War, Bamileke planters, led by the Kumsze Traditional Assembly of the Bamileke People under Mathias Djoumessi, began to plant coffee without authorization in a bold act of civil disobedience.[94] In an effort

---

[93] See Jean-Louis Dongmo, *Le dynamisme bamileke: La maîtrise de l'espace agraire*, Vol. I, CEPER: Yaoundé, 1981, 127-31; Ndobegang M. Mbapndah, "French Colonial Agricultural Policy, African Chiefs, and Coffee Growing in the Cameroun Grassfields, 1920-1960," *The International Journal of African Historical Studies* 27 (1994): 41-58 for more information on the cultivation of cash crops and food crops as affected by French administrative policy.

[94] See chaps. 2 and 3.

to appease the population, French administrators revoked the decree in 1947. Thereafter:

> *Anyone can grow coffee and as much as he wants. Coffee invades all the best land. The fact that coffee is practically the only source of revenue for the peasants and [since] the prices are increasing it makes the movement all the more irresistible.*[95]

In 1949, women of the Bamileke and Bamun districts requested complete freedom to grow coffee and to sell produce wherever they wished.[96] In 1949, the *Comité féminin* indicated that "anyone" did not include women, although women in the Grassfields were solely responsible for the production of food crops for domestic consumption.[97] In order to achieve economic independence Bamileke women requested that the UN support them in coffee-growing. Since the administration had already relaxed its control over coffee cultivation, the obstacle faced by Bamileke women must have been none other than male planters. In this instance, then, the

---

[95] Dongmo, *L'espace agraire*, 129.

[96] Petition from the Comité féminin de l'UPC concerning the Cameroons under French and British administration, 20 Nov 1949, UNTC, T/PET. 4/32.

[97] Miriam Goheen, *Men Own the Fields, Women Own the Crops: Gender and Power in the Cameroon Grassfields*, Madison, 1996, 66, 72-3, 84-5. Goheen explains that at the time of the petitions, the men of the western Grassfields attempted to prevent women from engaging in trade in public markets, even of "food crops." At the same time, women's production of food crops allowed men to produce commercial crops such as coffee that provided them with a cash income as well as increased social status. According to Goheen, who writes about the present day Northwest province, this resulted in a sharp gender divide, placing men and their activities in the public sphere where they had a greater degree of political access, while keeping women in the private sphere, far from the realm of politics and power.

women's petition contained a challenge to patriarchal dominance more than to the French administration.

Women in the Mungo region described the administration's taxation of the "sale of fresh provisions: macabo, plantains and yams," as "the pretext of a periodic market tax."[98] This tax, which extracted 200 to 500 CFA from women agriculturalists, constituted a "barbarous act which threaten[ed] the welfare of the women of Manjo in general ... a situation which threatened the future of women and made the family bankrupt."[99] Mrs. Julienne Nana, writing on behalf of the Women's Assembly of One Kamerun, presented women farmers as performing labor for the good of the society:

It must be recognized that macabo, yams, plantain and palm kernels are basic crops essential to the life of man, principles which arouse the conscience of man, fortify his spirit, elevate his moral ideas and improve his intelligence and make available to him the material fruits of women's work.[100]

The administration, by taxing the "fruits of the field," interfered in the sale of crops and thus established its dominance of the exchange between women farmers and the consumer.

As petitions from women farmers in the Mungo and Bamileke regions increased, UDEFEC membership most

---

[98] Petition from "One Kamerun," Assembly of the Regional Headquarters of the Kamerunian women, Manjo Sector, Concerning the Cameroons under French administration, 13 July 1958, T/PET.5/1345.
[99] Ibid.
[100] Petition from "One Kamerun" Assembly of the Regional Headquarter of the Kamerunian women, Manjo Sector, Concerning the Cameroons under French administration, 13 July 1958, T/PET.5/1345.

likely spread easily along the social networks created by agricultural patterns in the region. Even before colonialism, women's access to land had served as a "household level network," forming "intergroup ties [that] were and are realized by women cultivating their food crops in the estates of various principal heirs." [101] Women's involvement in various land plots beyond their husbands' holdings created specific links between households and villages that supported the economic interests of women by providing them with networks spread over a vast territory. The networks provided women with significant symbolic capital and allowed them to invest in circles of generosity and cooperation among relatives and neighbors. [102] Along these channels already in place, UDEFEC disseminated its message, particularly as it supported the role of women as crop producers.

As the number of petitions increased beginning in late 1954, a divergence in the narratives of women nationalists emerged. The leaders, mostly urbanites, employed a Western moral code to appeal to readers in the international sphere. The language used by rural women and women laborers contained fewer references to a Western or international political sphere, but was rich with symbols and codes rooted in local – or "traditional" – political culture and thus adapted the nationalist narratives to their own milieus. Petitioners at the local level cited personal grievances, followed by a claim,

---

[101] J. H. B. den Ouden, "Incorporation and Changes in the Composite Household. The Effects of Coffee Introduction and Food Crop Commercialization in Two Bamileke Chiefdoms, Cameroon," in C. Presvelou and S. Spijkers-Zwart eds., *The Household, Women and Agricultural Development*, Wageningen, 1980, 44-5.

[102] Ibid. This manner of networking continues today. Women rely heavily on these networks at times, such as during prolonged illness, after childbirth, or during seasons of heavy labor.

at times seemingly disjointed, for independence and unification. The women presented themselves as the victims of the wars of May 1955, told of losing their husbands to death or prison, and enumerated losses of property and material possessions. They asked for the UN's intervention and independence to deliver them from the "jaws of the lion, Roland Pré."[103]

By collectively recognizing each other's grievances as they gathered to compose and sign (or fingerprint) the petitions, the women of UDEFEC partook in a unifying ritual. They began to place their personal suffering - dislocated families, imprisoned husbands, finances devastated by destroyed property or arbitrary fines - within a larger context. Individual burdens became communal, as others acknowledged that "it could be my husband in jail next." The act of petitioning became a significant part of these local meetings, promoting a sense of solidarity that reached beyond the boundaries of the participants' own small village. The act of petitioning inherently promoted the UPC's nationalist project, even as it brought the specific grievances of a local population before the supervisory UN.

In 1956, Chrestine Emachoua composed a petition to the UN that demonstrated the difference in narratives of urban and rural petitioners:

Sir: When I left for Bafang with a bundle of wood,
they beat me and took my wood away from me
without reason.
They did the same when I had a basket of

---

[103] See Goheen, 74, 84, 88 and Pamela Feldman-Savelsberg, *Plundered Kitchens, Empty Wombs: Threatened Reproduction and Identity in the Cameroon Grassfields,* Ann Arbor, 1999, 125.

cassava.

They beat me and took away a basket of
cassava meal without reason.

When I was carrying a basket of macabo, they
sent the police, beat me, and took away the
macabo.

When I had a basket of taro, they sent it to the
police and it was the same story.

When I fell sick. I was taken to the dispensary,
where I was given no treatment. When a woman
gives birth at the dispensary, they give the baby an
injection to kill it.

I haven't much to tell you.

Long live the United Nations!

Long live a unified and independent
Cameroons!

Emachoua Chrestine[104]

Mrs. Emachoua's petition must have sounded strange to members of the Trusteeship Council, but it succinctly expressed the symbolism of the local moral order. According to her, the administration "ate"[105] all of her food and took away her means of supporting herself and her family. Even

---

[104] Petition from Mrs. Chrestine Emachoua concerning the Cameroons under French administration, Baboucha, 13 Dec 1956, T/PET.5/1112.

[105] Here I use the term "eat" in the sense defined by J.-F. Bayart's "*la politique du ventre*" which implies both a style of governing which preys on its subjects and their resources, and a link in the imaginary between "eating" and power. The metaphor has become common in the literature: see also Peter Geschiere, *The Modernity of Witchcraft: Politics and the Occult in Postcolonial Africa*, Charlottesville, 1997 and Michael G. Schatzberg, "Power, Legitimacy and 'Democratisation' in Africa," *Africa* 63.4 (1993): 445-61. Geschiere and Schatzberg extend the metaphor, linking "eating" and power to witchcraft the occult in the imaginary.

the medical treatment offered by the administration was suspected of causing further misfortune.[106] Mrs. Emachoua told of an administration that not only stripped her of her means of subsistence, but also offered nothing in return. As expressed in Mrs. Emachoua's closing statement, the rejection of colonialist ideology became perhaps most visible in women's perceptions of European bio-medicine, which they increasingly perceived as threatening, if not pernicious, to the well-being of Cameroonian society.

The "Perimeter of Death:"[107] Pernicious Bio-medicine, Assaults on Fertility, and the Unburied Dead

From the early days of UDEFEC, its founders stressed the importance of medical care for women, particularly antenatal care, and the need for improved maternity ward facilities. This emphasis merged with the principles advocated by the WIDF and other international NGO's at the International Conference for the Defence of the Child held in Vienna in 1952, attended by representatives of UDEFEC.[108] The importance of child-bearing and maternity care resonated with Cameroonian women in urban and rural areas alike.[109] As seen in Mrs. Emachoua's petition, many women may have perceived the French administration's threats to agricultural fertility to extend into the realm of biological fertility as

---

[106] See Mbembe "Domaines."

[107] The phrase is from Mbembe, "Domaines."

[108] See chap. 2.

[109] It is possible that women bearing children felt more vulnerable to possible complications in child-birth during times of political crisis, such as the widespread repression of UPC and UDEFEC members launched by the French administration. See Feldman-Savelsberg, *Plundered Kitchens*, for a historicized anthropological account of the changing significance of fertility in Bangangte society, in the Bamileke region.

well.[110] These fears were expressed in the petitions received by the UN, which contained many references to the administration's abuse of pregnant women that often caused miscarriages, and administrators' disregard for the well-being of Cameroonian children or babies.

In June 1955, after the French administration banned the popular parties, women decried the repression faced by women, again focusing on pregnant women and their young children. Marthe Moumié wrote that Roland Pré attempted to:

'divide the Africans' which has led to Cameroonian bloodshed. Eighteen injured at Bafoussam, 5 at Meinganga, half a dozen at Garoua, and a woman who miscarried owing to those threats...[111]

Furthermore, petitioners complained that after the members of UPC and UDEFEC had to flee into the *maquis*, "nursing mothers feed their babies in disease-ridden forests... Children die of malnutrition or parasitic diseases," [112] "mothers dragged along their very young children or

---

[110] Although Cameroonians did not reject European bio-medicine altogether, the conflict over its uses had to do with their distrust of European medical personnel's intent. As Luise White points out in her work on regional understandings of bio-medicine in eastern Africa, Cameroonian women struggled to control "the context in which cultural and biomedical contact took place." Luise White, *Speaking with Vampires: Rumor and History in Colonial Africa*, Berkeley, 1999, 104. As the anti-colonial movement grew, so did the distrust of European medical institutions until they began to be perceived as potentially harmful to Cameroonian society.

[111] Petition from the Editorial Board of the Newspaper *Femmes camerounaises* concerning the Cameroons under French administration, 7 June 1955, T/PET.5/618.

[112] Petition from the WIDF, 25 Oct 1955, Berlin, T/PET.5/818.

abandoned them like orphans in their huts."[113] After the UPC launched a successful boycott of the elections of December 1956,[114] Marthe Ouandié telegraphed the UN from Kumba to alert it that the French government had brought "thousands of troops parachutists" into the Sanaga-Maritime region who "are ruthlessly murdering pregnant women and babies."[115] Siewe Hileine wrote from the Bafang region in 1957:

> *while the men are away in the bush [fleeing the arrests by the administration, the French colonialists come and maltreat women, untold numbers of whom have been killed, including some who were pregnant.*[116]

As conflicts in the Bamileke region escalated, numerous petitions to the UN cited rape as a weapon wielded by soldiers under French command in a blatant assault on the bodies and fertility of women:

> *Since 21 March 1957 the French Government has been bringing in thousands of soldiers from all the neighbouring colonies and.... in the Bamileke region in particular, the authorities have the*

---

[113] Petition from Marie-Irène Ngapeth, 20 June 1955, Kumba, T/PET.5/913.

[114] The progressive parties organized the boycott to protest France's "establishment of a fake Legislative Assembly as well as an Executive Council with the purpose of integrating the Kamerun in the French Union." According to French records, 55% of the voting population abstained from going to the polls; according to the UPC records, 75% of the population boycotted. See UPC, *The Kamerun*, 11. At UDEFEC meetings in the Babimbi region, members were told not to go to the polls.

[115] Petition from Mrs. Marthe Ouandié concerning the Cameroons under British administration, Kumba, 4 Jan 1957, T/PET.5/1010.

[116] Petition from Siewe Hileine, Member of the UDEFEC Committee, Moumée, 19 Feb 1957, T/PET.5/1108.

wives of political prisoners and maquisards *raped, each woman by ten soldiers...*[117]

Rumors began to be circulated that women prisoners were subject to the most heinous forms of torture. According to reports of petitioners, Marthe Bahida "was arrested, beaten with clubs and horribly tortured; her genitals were burnt with a red hot iron."[118] Mrs. Siewe expressed the growing perception that any alternative would be preferable to the present fate of Cameroonians under the French administration: "Frankly, anyone killed here in the Cameroons is better off than those still alive and enduring the sufferings inflicted on us by the French colonialists."[119]

Demonstrating a recognition that France had promised to uphold and protect the rights and well-being of Cameroonian women and children, women of UDEFEC wrote that, in fact, children in the territory were not safe from the violence unleashed by the French administration:

---

[117] Thirty-nine petitions concerning the dissolution of the three organizations in the Cameroons under British administration and repressive measures in the Bamileke region of the Cameroons under French administration, 12 Sept 1957, T/PET.4&5/20. Out of the 39 petitions recorded, four contained references to the rape of Bamileke women. Other petitions refer to rape in the Bamileke region. For example, 45 Petitions, 5 Feb 1958, T/PET.5/1312: "[At Bandenkop] there are more than 2, 000 soldiers who commit all kinds of inhumane barbarities, raping little girls eight and nine years old." Near Bafoussam, "women were ... taken to the army camp where more than 110 soldiers violated a single woman and when she was nearly dead she was automatically burned or thrown into the water." Petition from Mrs. Marie Mowolio, housewife, Bamendjida region, Mbouda Subdivision, via Bamenda, PO Box 20, 21 June 1957, T/PET.5/1287.

[118] Petition from the WIDF, 14 Oct 1955, T/PET.5/818.

[119] Petilion from Siewe Hileine, Member of the UDEFEC Committee, Moumée, 19 Feb 1957, T/PET.5/1108.

[I]n its promises, which never go any further than the halls of the UN, the French Government undertook to care for our children, but the contrary is happening for the French police come into our homes and maltreat our children, as in the case of little Bodo Itot who was beaten on 25 March 1956 while he was holding his tiny brother, who is hardly five months old, in his arms. The infant was thrown to the ground.[120]

Gertrude Omog wrote that during the events of May 1955, those members of the UPC, the JDC, and UDEFEC held at the central police station after their arrest were

subjected to terrible tortures by officers of the French judicial police, that is, by officers of the law aware of the heinous crimes they were committing, especially against women, including the mother of an infant.[121]

She continued, implying the complicity of the Catholic missions in carrying out the French administration's project of exterminating:

all honest citizens so that the next [UN Visiting] Mission will find them dead and will not have adequate evidence on which to condemn Roland Pré's policy. At Loum, it was a French priest, Father Bernard, who fired upon two people, one of them a pregnant woman, and killed them instantly; he then went to the school where he fired upon children.[122]

---

[120] Petition from Libong Local Committee of UDEFEC, meeting in Plenary Assembly on 19 Nov 1956, T/PET.5.1223.
[121] Petition from Mrs Gertrude Omog, *maquis*, 14 June 1955, T/PET.5/674.
[122] Ibid.

The petitions further indicated that women viewed the medical care provided by the French administration that apparently cared so little for the health and well-being of Cameroonian children to be at best ineffective, and at worst, harmful.

Cameroonian women believed European medical institutions to offer "inferior treatment," which was "likely greatly to reduce the population." [123] Women found the maternity wards available to be severely inadequate as expressed by Marthe Moumié in her piece published in *Femmes camerounaises* in 1955: "African women (especially Cameroonians) give birth on the bare ground in the lying-in centres, and that gives rise to a high rate of infant mortality." [124] Martha Ngo Mayag wrote from Douala in November 1954: "Our maternity homes, which differ greatly from those provided for European women, entirely fail to safeguard the life of the mother or the new-born child."[125] A petition from the Society of the Women of Bomp described the conditions of the maternity wards in greater detail:

> *In the Dibang dispensary, which has just been built by the sweat of our husbands' brows, the treatment of maternity cases is appalling. Women in labour are not given the slightest help.*[126]

---

[123] Petition from Aguemani Elisabeth, Bafia, 30 Aug 1956, T/PET.5/949.

[124] Petition from the Editorial Board of the Newspaper, *Femmes camerounaise*s, concerning the Cameroons under French administration, 7 June 1955, T/PET.5/618.

[125] Petition from Martha Ngo Mayag, 12 Nov 1954, New-Bell, Douala, T/PET.5/502.

[126] Petition from the Société des femmes Bomp, UPC Local Committee to the Visiting Mission, received 25 June 1956, T/PET.5/894, Section II.

Nevertheless, the French administration stipulated that all birthing women had to come to the new dispensary, thereby eliminating women's ability to choose alternate methods of birthing. The women of Bomp perceived this effort to control their birthing methods as detrimental to their health and to that of their newborn children:

As soon as they built the Dibang dispensaries, they forbade us to have our babies anywhere in the village other than the dispensary. There were cases of still-births. A room of three-square meters is used to accommodate ten new mothers. Look at the diseases our newborn babies catch: whooping cough, worms, scabies [sic], yaws, and muscle weakness. Since then, newborn babies, who need every care, have had to spend the night on a rough board. Only our husbands, by their efforts, manage to make bamboo beds for ourselves and our children.[127]

The petition ended with an emphatic appeal to be allowed to manage their own maternity and natal care, since the facilities provided by the French administration were so inadequate:

Is it right that a woman in childbirth should not be attended by a doctor? For us, Cameroonian women living in rural areas, it would be better to have our babies in the village rather than to go and have our children die at the hospital.[128]

In the Bafang region, women petitioners also demonstrated their mistrust of the medical facilities and care provided by the French. In early 1957, a series of petitions

---

[127] Ibid.
[128] Ibid.

came into the UN expressing concern over the injections given to children in the region. Mrs. Passa Tchaffi and Mrs. Agathe Matene wrote: "the French ... have prepared injections and put schoolchildren into a hut, where they gave them these shots to weaken their minds."[129] Mrs. Rose Marie Mouna in the Bafang subdivision wrote: "On October 1956, France prepared medicaments with which to inject schoolchildren; the shots drove the children mad."[130] Mrs. Elisabeth Aguemani believed that "the most scientific French men have infected all the dogs in the Cameroons by means of injections and all these mad dogs have now bitten almost 100 per 1,000 of the total population of the Cameroons."[131] Mrs. Emachoua wrote: "When a woman gives birth at the dispensary, they give the baby an injection to kill it."[132] The women's distrust of the medical practices introduced by a French administration underscored differences between indigenous and European perceptions of medicine. Women, dissatisfied with or alarmed by European institutions of medicine, particularly those associated with antenatal and child care, identified with one another in the denunciation of this foreign medical intrusion.[133]

---

[129] Petition from Mrs. Passa Tchaffi, Chairman of the UDEFEC Committee at Bafang and Mrs. Agathe Matene, received 20 Feb 1957, T/PET.5/1109.

[130] Petition from Mrs. Rose Marie Mouna concerning the Cameroons under French Administration, received 20 Feb 1957, T/PET.5/1113.

[131] Petition from Elisabeth Aguemani, Bafia, 30 Aug 1956, T/PET.5/949.

[132] Petition from Mrs. Chrestine Emachoua concerning the Cameroons under French administration, Baboucha, 13 Dec 1956, T/PET.5/112.

[133] For a different interpretation of bio-medicine's impact on anti-colonialist ideas, see Megan Vaughan, *Curing their Ills: Colonial Power and African Illness*, Stanford, 1991, 204-5. For a historical interpretation of rumors about injections circulating in colonial East and Central Africa, see White, *Vampires*, chap. 3.

The emphasis on the administration's threat to fertility accompanied the UPC's ideology that equated the colonial regime with death and illness. Achille Mbembe writes that in the ideology of southern Cameroon, particularly in the Sanaga-Maritime region, sickness was considered to be a symbol of disharmony both for the individual and for the society. Sickness indicated the presence of misfortune. According to Mbembe, colonialism was perceived as an illness, "devouring" social ties, and "swallowing" vital parts of a person.[134]

For women, such vital parts certainly included their reproductive capacity. At UDEFEC meetings in Babimbi, women were told that the administration wanted to exterminate all members of the nationalist movements and that European bio-medicine served their purpose:

Whites came to Cameroon for no other reason than to cheat blacks... The Doctor infects us with all sorts of sicknesses. For us dying is as common as shitting; this is what decreases the population so they can uproot our liberation movement.[135]

---

[134] Mbembe, "Domaines," 107. Mbembe analyses the dreams of Ruben Um Nyobé during his period in the *maquis*, explaining that they are a symbol of the Bassa ideology that made sense of the visible world in the invisible, that is the world of dreams, the night, death, and the world of the "double" -- a state of being two persons at once, one visible, and one invisible, the latter having the ability to "see" in the invisible world. Many of Um Nyobé's dreams were about comrades who had been killed coming back to visit him and give him advice. Mbembe thus presents Um Nyobé as mediator between the two worlds, the visible and the invisible, and demonstrates his key role in reshaping members' symbolic order to reject the ideology of colonialism and adhere to a local ideology - one that would include the invisible.

[135] Marie-Anne Nsoga to UDEFEK meeting held at the home of MBOK Souzanne, 6 Dec 1956, Babimbi.

The birthing centers, which gathered mothers and their newborns under their control, were perceived as the ideal place for the administration to carry out its project of thwarting the nationalist movement by eliminating a second generation of nationalists. In June 1958, several petitions informed the UN that: "More than 45 women suffered miscarriages in the Adlucem hospital of the Bakar Bafang Catholic Mission which is run by Thérèse Gasteau." [136] Women recognized that the disappearance of their husbands, whether they had fled into the *maquis* or had been arrested or killed, threatened biological fertility as well. Poline Matachange, a farmer from Bamendje, wrote, "Since 1955 the women of Kamerun no longer give birth, you know well that a hen can lay eggs only if she has been with the cock. We women of Kamerun want to have back our husbands."[137]

Members of UDEFEC viewed the European administration as disseminating ill health and death and threatening fertility, and equated the achievement of independence with a restoration of health and well-being. UDEFEC leaders promised that with independence would come restored health for Cameroonian women:

> *I tell you, dear friends, that countries that have their independence have civilization. There, pregnant women are well treated... I beg you, friends, bear the condemnation, the maquis, and*

---

[136] Fifty-three petitions containing complaints relating to various repressive measures in the Cameroons under French Administration, 5 Nov 1958. T/PET.5/1351. Three of these petitions referred to miscarriages at the Adlucem hospital.
[137] Petition from Poline Matachange, farmer, Central Quarter, Bamendje to President of the 13th Session of the UN, 10 Dec 1958, T/PET.5/1399.

the other burdens without giving up in order to obtain immediate
independence for our Kamerun.[138]

UDEFEC provided women with a symbolic inoculation against colonialism's "codification of symbols," that is, it served Cameroonian women as a weapon in the "struggle over meaning" that was taking place during the ideological conflict between the European administrations and members of the popular movements. [139] As Cameroonian women rejected European medical institutions, they refused the administrations' definition of physical and social well-being, replacing it with their own.

Educational institutions became another symbolic battleground. The school system, such as it existed in rural areas, represented another space of European control over the formation of Cameroonian children. In 1949, the *Comité féminin* of the UPC had written that the shortage of schools condemned Cameroonian children to ignorance, constituting a serious obstacle for the prospects of women to take part "in the work of emancipating our country."[140] In 1952, the first UDEFEC petition on record deplored the lack of schools that caused over half the children of school age to go without schooling. In 1955, a petition from the Babimbi branch of UDEFEC commented on the irrelevance of colonial education:

The children learn nothing but passages from plays written centuries ago by Molière and no teaching is given on indigenous

---

[138] Ernestine Mouthamal to UDEFEC meeting, 7 Dec 1956.

[139] See Mbembe, "Domaines," 97.

[140] Petition from the *Comité féminin* de l'UPC concerning the Cameroons under French and British administration, 20 Nov 1949, UNTC, T/PET.4/32.

history, or customary and traditional dancing; the children only learn the history of distant countries so that a child who can recite details of the map of France does not know the name of a river flowing through his own village.[141]

Mrs. Penda's request for an educational curriculum that included "subjects relating to our country, language, history, and dances" demonstrated UDEFEC women's understanding that foreign dominance must be combated on cultural grounds.

Women from Bafang repeatedly complained of the Catholic mission's shortcomings in schooling. In 1954, the UDEFEC local committee at Fonkouakem wrote:

When the priests, those practised members of the elite of the colonialist machine in our Cameroons, those people who blaze the trail for the colonialists, say that they will set up a children's school in the village, it is merely to increase poverty. The very first day a child goes to the school, he is made to pay 400-500 francs, according to his age, and within two days he is thrown out.[142]

In December 1954, another petition from the Bafang region, composed at the UPC's General Assembly, accused the head of the Momé Catholic Mission of using his school as a form of forced labor:

We ask the head of the church whether Father Pierre of the Momé Catholic Mission really left France to organize forced labour

---

[141] Petition from Marthe Penda, Secretary of the Babimbi branch of UDEFEC, 13 Dec l954, Ngambe, T/PET.5/409.
[142] Petition from UDEFEC at Fonkouakem, Bafang region, 22 Nov 1954, T/PET.5/512.

in the Cameroons or to serve their God. Twenty-four pupils were
expelled by Father Pierre because they did not turn up for work on
Mr. Meleyou's plantation. The only reason why a few boys are still
there is because they signed contracts for the plantations at Momé.[143]

In the British Cameroons, petitioning women stressed the
lack of education, arguing for its importance in providing
their children with opportunities:

There is no free school, following the Universal Declaration of
Human Rights, Article 26.[144] *Without education children are*
destined to be plantation workers just like their father.[145]

Responding to the need to educate Cameroonians to the
political situation, presidents of the regional and local
meetings in the Babimbi region devoted themselves to
fulfilling their role as educators of the "masses," thereby
replacing the European curriculum.[146] Marie-Anne Nsoga
instructed the directors of the local committees to consider
themselves the teachers and catechists of the people:

---

[143] Petition from the General Assembly of the UPC held at Bafang, 5 Dec
1954, T/PET.5/410.

[144] Article 26: 1. Everyone has the right to education. Education shall be
free, at least in the elementary and fundamental stages. ... 2. Education
shall be directed to the full development of the human personality and to
the strengthening of respect for human rights and fundamental freedoms.

[145] Petition from Mrs. Theresia Nana, President of the Women's
Committee of One Kamerun, Tiko, 5 Nov 1958, T/PET.4/156.

[146] Ruben Um Nyobé sent out a tract to the UPC, JDC and UDEFEC
leaders on 20 Sept 1955, stipulating the methods for re-organizing in the
maquis. He stressed the importance of local committees in educating the
members in attendance. Ruben Um Nyobé, *Problème national kamerunais,*
Paris, 1984, 320.

So I'm speaking to the directors of the local committees, they are the ones that assemble the people and educate them, I rely on you to be patient and to work for the masses.[147]

When spreading the news of the planned boycott of the December 1956 elections, Mrs. Nsoga told UDEFEC members in Babimbi that their political role was as important as that of the women in urban centers:

The December 1956 vote: it's a French ambush, you shouldn't vote. Douala, Yaoundé, Eséka have passed their votes, but here in Babimbi, we are in the bush, uneducated, what should we do? Be united, and distance yourselves from the colonialists and their lackeys. UDEFEC hires [148] *all militant activists and leaders of the organization to work together, fraternally. UDEFEC denounces tribalism, power struggles, etc...*[149]

Even as the women of UDEFEC wrote petitions exposing the lack of education, the party attempted to awaken the people to the political situation in the territory, instructing them on what they could do to achieve liberation from foreign domination.

After the French administration banned the progressive parties in July 1955, followed by the British in June 1957, it became clear to remaining members in the *maquis* that their struggle for independence would be carried out on the

---

[147] Réunion du 15 Nov 1956 sur la proposition de la délégation d'UDEFEC au domicile du camarade Yedna Madeleine, Comité local, Mabenge.

[148] The UN translator may have translated the word "*engage*" as "hires" here, whereas "calls upon" may be more accurate, given the context.

[149] Réunion du 6 Dec 1956, UDEFEK, à la maison de Mbok Souzanne.

"perimeter of death."[150] With the leaders in exile,[151] hiding out in the forest, or in prison, the remaining members of the progressive parties lived in a state of perpetual fear that they would be rounded up, imprisoned, or executed.[152] Petitions flowed in with references to death, extermination, execution, drowning, and unexpected ambushes, searches, intrusions into private homes, and violations of privacy. In July 1955, the UDEFEC committee of Douala wrote: "Bands of soldiers continue to search the Cameroonian forests in order to arrest and kill members of the UPC."[153] Marie-Irène Ngapeth, after the May riots in 1955, wrote:

---

[150] See Mbembe, "Domaines," 108-121.

[151] Petition from Mr. Félix Moumié concerning the Cameroons under British administration, Victoria, 4 June 1957, T/PET.4/141. Moumié wrote that "Unikamerun" had been declared illegal in Western Kamerun and Nigeria. Eleven of the leaders were under arrest at Victoria, "pending deportation [to the] country of their choice." They had chosen Sudan, Libya, Liberia, or Ghana. Moumié requested the UN to obtain authorization for the UPC and UDEFEC leaders to enter those countries and to alert the UN Refugee and Human Rights divisions.

[152] The French "pacification" forces rounded up the population of entire villages in the Sanaga-Maritime, searched homes for incriminating documents such as UPC tracts or meeting records and arrested anyone accused of being associated with the party. Mbembe, "Pouvoir" and interviews. See also Um Nyobé, *Problème*, 350-1 for his account of the French "pacification" of the Sanaga-Maritime. See UPC, *La tutelle international à l'épreuve*, Cairo 1959, 69-72 for an extensive list of "concentration camps, prisons, military posts, destroyed villages, houses set on fire, etc." The list is arranged by subdivision. See UPC, *The UPC Denounces the Planned Systematic Tortures in the Kamerun,* Cairo, 1958, for similar lists, including the names of those arrested, and lengthy descriptions of the conditions in the prisons. The National Archives in Yaoundé contain descriptions of the prisons, written by prisoners while incarcerated. See for example, UPC, detention, 1955, 1 AC 1977, ANY.

[153] Petition from the Committee of UDEFEC, 13 July 1955, Douala, T/PET.5/742.

Fernando-Poo authorities reported to have found bullet-riddled corpses in the sea, which suggests that those who were killed during those black nights were thrown into the Wouri, the nights being too short to bury them all.[154]

In the Bamileke region the Central Committees of UDEFEC met at Kumba[155] and wrote:

some 75 percent of our women are without their husbands now, for some of the men are in prison and others are in the maquis outside the territory whither they have been driven by the severity of the local authorities... We are driven to despair when we find the corpses of our husbands, who were imprisoned, thrown into creeks as was the case with Mr. Massanga, who was arrested at Mbouda on 28 August 1956 and killed on 15 September 1956.[156]

A publication from the Foreign Delegation of the UPC in Cairo, signed by Felix Moumié and Ernest Ouandié in July 1958 described the discovery of bodies "found floating in the water, bodies which belonged to patriots who were thought to have been deported to unknown destinations." [157] The publication listed by name the "patriots" whose bodies were found in the Midom River located between Batié and Foumban on 29 November 1957. Ten of the men killed and thrown into the river came from Bayangam, four from

---

[154] Petition from Marie-Irène Ngapeth, Kumba, 20 June 1955, T/PET.5/913.

[155] Marie-Anne Nsoga, president of the regional delegation of UDEFEC in Babimbi, oversaw elections at which UDEFEC members in Babimbi chose representatives to attend this General Assembly of UDEFEC Central Committees at Kumba.

[156] Petition from UDEFEC General Assembly, Bamileke Region, 10 Nov 1956, T/PET.5/984.

[157] UPC, *Tortures*, 36.

Bandenkop, one from Bangou, and five were identified as "traditional chiefs" from the Mbouda subdivision.[158] The French administration eventually posted soldiers by the waterways to prevent the retrieval of bodies.[159] A telegram from Marthe Ouandié protested that the "French Government is resolved to exterminate [the] entire population" in the Sanaga-Maritime, and that "Thousands [of] unburied corpses [are] rotting beside roads."[160]

The proximity to death of the party members in the internal exile of the *maquis* contributed to the creation of a new, nationalist ideology. In the south of Cameroon, the dead were believed to follow currents of water downstream, as did the invisible "doubles" of people in the visible world.[161] The recurrence of images of dead bodies in water reinforced the population's equation of colonial rule with death, demonstrating that, as Mbembe suggests, the UPC-led revolt and the European suppression thereof involved a struggle over the symbolic and the invisible, as much as the material. The administration that imposed death did not suppress the

[158] Ibid., 37. Marc Michel and Jean-François Bayart frame the conflict in the Bamileke region in terms of "traditional elders" vs. popular insurgents comprised of *cadets sociaux*. See Michel, 251-57 and Jean-François Bayart, *L'Etat au Cameroun* [1979], Paris, 1985, 42-44 and 64-68. However, my interview with Marcel Ngandjong Feze, Chief of Badenkop (see chap. 4, above), the UPC publications and petitions in the UN records suggest that the conflict had less to do with hierarchical authority than with anti-colonial aspirations. The French deposed or forced into exile pro-UPC chiefs, and replaced them with "puppet" chiefs who sought to benefit from their collaboration with the French administration. See also Meredith Terretta, "Chiefs, Traitors and Representatives: The Construction of a Political Repertoire in Independence Era Cameroun," *International Journal of African Historical Studies* 43.2 (2010): 227-58.
[159] UPC, *Tortures*, 37.
[160] Petition from Mrs. Marthe Ouandié concerning the Cameroons under British administration, Kumba, 30 Dec 1956, T/PET.5/1010, Add. 2.
[161] Mbembe, "Domaines," 118.

nationalist movement. Instead it provided fuel for its fire, particularly in the Sanaga-Maritime. In Bassa societies, no death is recognized unless it is explained and those responsible for it are identified. Although the French administration proved itself capable of the elimination and disposal of physical bodies, it could not impose a cultural acceptance of death, particularly for those bodies that did not receive a proper burial but drifted away in the waterways.[162] Those inhabitants of the Sanaga-Maritime were moved by a desire to explain the deaths of the "unburied dead," and to challenge and punish those responsible for them, thereby allowing them to pass into the ancestral world. As it was, the unresolved deaths of the nationalists exacerbated political upheavals in the region.

Conclusion

The petitions of UDEFEC women exposed the full spectrum of the movement against foreign administration - from the most intimate space of childbirth and bio-medicine, to the economic terrain of markets and farms. By bringing the movement into these spaces, Cameroonian women led the way in redefining the political terms framing the opposition between nationalists and colonialists. Rejecting the narrow confines for politics outlined by French

---

[162] Mbembe's analysis of death in Bassa societies focuses on the death of Um Nyobé. Since Um Nyobé's death was not properly explained, his people were unable to facilitate his transition from the world of the living to the ancestral world. His death was left unresolved, and he was "badly buried." This has caused unrest in the political community of Cameroon, and for Mbembe, Um Nyobé serves as a symbol of the post-colonial state, which rests uneasily along the fault lines of unfulfilled political aspirations. See Mbembe, "Pouvoir," 225-28.

administrators encouraging political collaboration, the UPC and UDEFEC taught their members that the political terrain extended into all areas of Cameroonian experience. Emphasizing the importance of Cameroonian culture, nationalists in the Bassa region and the Bamileke region alike criticized the imposition of a European curriculum on school-aged children. By launching a transregional attack on European medical institutions, women petitioners expressed their fears that Europeans had adopted an ad hoc policy of curing the country of nationalist influence by exterminating babies, school children, pregnant women, and the elderly.

The British and French increased their repression of the progressive movements' members, even as their ideology solidified, contributing to the widening gap between the two sides. The only relief for the popular parties would come with the departure of the European administrations. Seen in these terms, it is not so difficult to understand why, following the exile of their leaders, remaining members of the progressive movements would risk their already precarious lives to force the withdrawal of Europeans from their territory.

Chapter 6

Conclusion
Towards a Nation of Outsiders

Tu n'es pas parti, et pourtant tu n'es pas là. / You haven't left and yet you are not here.[1]

The military repression of the nationalists proved particularly violent, particularly after the UPC attempted to organize a territory-wide boycott of the December 1956 elections and created the *Comité national d'organisation* (CNO) to enforce the boycott in the Sanaga-Maritime.[2] Outlawed, the party had no political recourse but to organize a boycott of the elections, which it depicted as the administration's ploy to finally integrate French Cameroon into the French Union. To vote or not to vote was, to Um Nyobé, a life or death question.[3] The *Zone de pacification* established in the Sanaga-Maritime led to the resettlement of the region's population along the roads,

---

[1] Song from Makaï referring to Ruben Um Nyobé after his assassination, as quoted in Achille Mbembe, "Pouvoir des morts et langage des vivants: Les errances de la mémoire nationaliste au Cameroun," in Jean-François Bayart, et al. eds., *Le politique par le bas: Contributions a une problématique de la démocratie*, Paris, 1992, 183-229, 226.

[2] Despite Ruben Um Nyobé's reluctance to use violence as a strategy for the liberation of Cameroonians from European dominance, the French dissolution of the territorial assembly in August 1956 and its scheduling of new elections for December 1956 without granting amnesty to UPC members pushed the movement to a choice between surrender, or radicalization. See Achille Mbembe, *La naissance du maquis dans le Sud-Cameroun, 1920-1960*, Paris, 1996, 328. Ruben Um Nyobé, *Problème national kamerunais*, Paris, 1984, 307, 317. The formation of the CNO in Makai, Eseka Subdivision, had as objective to isolate and threaten the valets, or those who supported the French administration's political tactics.

[3] Ruben Um Nyobé, *Ecrits sous maquis*, Paris, 1989, 173-174.

125

while marketplaces were abolished, and crops destroyed and pillaged to prevent their sustenance of the *maquisards*. The French administration attempted to combat the nationalist movement's popularity by disseminating anti-UPC ideology, imitating the UPC and UDEFEC grassroots strategies. The administration recruited traitors to the movement to act as "catechists" to the people, sending them out to tell anti-UPC parables at public gatherings, the morals of which could be summed up in proverbs.[4] These strategies, referred to by the administration as "psychological actions undertaken by the Administration in 1958 to turn the masses against the UPC,"[5] met with ridicule, or were reinterpreted by listeners to illustrate the importance of the UPC or the independence of the population of the Bassa region. The administration's efforts to re-appropriate the imaginary[6] - that is the symbols, narratives, modes of expression, and behaviors of nationalists - proved futile. Perhaps, considering Bassa women nationalists' role in awakening the peoples' political consciousness, the administrators would have had more success if they had selected women to serve as their primary propagandists.

In the Bamileke region, the administration focused its military attacks on villages with pro-UPC chiefs. The administrative strategy for stifling the movement's popularity in the Bamileke region was to:

---

[4] Mbembe, *Naissance*, 364-376.

[5] Ibid.

[6] For Mbembe, revolutions in Africa belong to the order of the imaginary. See Achille Mbembe, "Domaines de la nuit et autorité onirique dans les maquis du Sud-Cameroun (1955-1958)," *Journal of African History* 31.1 (1991): 89-121, 89-93, and *Naissance*, 362, chap. 12, and Conclusion.

arrest the Chief and take him to Dschang, where the local authority immediately replaced him without more ado, by a chief of its own choice, contrary to the wishes and the tradition of the people of that chiefdom.[7]

Such was the fate of Pierre Kamdem Ninyim, the Chief of Baham, whose arrest was protested by UPC and UDEFEC members even beyond the Bamileke region.[8] That Bamileke women wrote in support of some chiefs, and described others as pawns of the French administration offers a new look at the nationalist party's place in Bamileke politics. The historical scholarship tends to explain the conflict in terms of a "traditional aristocracy" versus the *cadets sociaux*, that is juniors, agriculturalists, laborers, and women.[9] Instead, the petitions suggest that the conflict had more to do with nationalist politics and alliances formed in support of or against the foreign administration in Yaoundé.

---

[7] Petition from Mr. Pierre Fayep, 26 Nov 1956, T/PET.5/998, protesting the arrest of the Chief of Baham on 22 Nov 1956; Petition from JDC, Local Branch of the Haoussa Quarter, Kumba, 26 Nov 1956 T/PET.5/991, protesting the arrest of Pierre Nyoum [sic], Chief of Baham, for refusing to "vote in favour of the loi-cadre;" Petition from Mrs. Gertrude Nguemdjo, Babete-Mbouda, c/o the Central Council of UDEFEC, Kumba, 9 Dec 1956, T/PET.5/1054. Complaints about chiefs acting as agents of the administration came from Petition from the people of Balessing, 24 Jan 1957, T/PET.5/1084, which described their Chief Tiogning as having "already become a French citizen."

[8] On the deposition of the Chief of Baham, Pierre Kamdem-Ninyim, in 1956, see Jean-François Bayart, *L'Etat au Cameroun* [1979], Paris, 1985, 64 and Victor Le Vine, "Leadership and Regime Changes in Perspective," in Michael Schatzberg and I. William Zartman. eds., *The Political Economy of Cameroon*, New York, 1986: 20-52. Ninyim was eventually granted amnesty, and was named Minister of Health in Ahidjo's government, only to be executed for treason in January of 1964.

[9] Bayart, *Cameroun*, 64.

Throughout the period of "pacification," petitions continued to pour into the UN. After the elections in December 1956, a series of telegrams flooded the Trusteeship Council from Kumba. Four of them came from Marthe Ouandié, asking the UN to ignore the results of the elections and alerting it to the number of troops being amassed in the Sanaga-Maritime and the thousands of "unburied corpses rotting beside roads."[10] Soon after the elections, on 3 June 1957, the British "under the instigation of the French imperialists have dissolved the UPC, the JDC, and UDEFEC without cause and have also deported 13 of the leaders of these institutions and confiscated their belongings."[11]

Recognizing the threat posed by the UN's support of human rights and realizing the significance of petitioning in promoting solidarity among nationalists, the administrations' penalties for communicating with the UN became increasingly severe. From 4 to 29 June 1957, immediately after the British ban on the nationalist movements and the arrest and forced deportation of the UPC, UDEFEC, and JDC leadership delegation from Kumba, the remaining local committees circulated 71 petitions in protest of the dissolution. [12] After banning the party in June 1957, the

---

[10] Petition from Mrs. Marthe Ouandié Concerning the Cameroons under British Administration, Kumba, 30 Dec 1956, T/PET.5/1010, 4 Jan 1957, T/PET.5/1010, Add. 1, 11 Jan 1957, T/PET.5/1010, Add. 2.

[11] UPC Foreign Delegation, *The Kamerun,* Cairo, 1957, 13. Among those deported were Abel Kingue, Roland Félix Moumié, and Emest Ouandié husband of Marthe Ouandié, a member of the executive committee of UDEFEC.

[12] Petitions came from petitioners in Bamenda, Douala, Tiko, and from those affiliated with various Associations of Cameroonian students in France and with the International League for the Rights of Man in New York. Seventy-one petitions concerning the dissolution of three organizations in the Cameroons under British Administration, 26 July 1957, T/PET.4/144.

British authorities occupied the offices of the UPC, UDEFEC, and the JDC, and attempted to strip the remaining members of their ability to petition:

All of the offices of the above-mentioned Movements have been spitefully stripped of their contents by the British authorities. Not a scrap of paper has been left. They removed all our property, such as cars, typewriters, Roneo machines [mimeographs], furniture, writing material, membership cards, badges, large sums of money, large bundles of paper, headed note-paper ... and a large number of documents.[13]

Petitioning became an act that warranted arrest by the British administration as it had in the French territory from 13 July 1955:

Since the morning of 5 June 1957 people sending cablegrams addressed to various destinations and describing the bloody events, massacres, terrorism, repressive measures and arrests, are arrested at the Bamenda post office and taken to the police station and then to prison.[14]

Even being caught with a copy of the Universal Declaration of Human Rights could be cause for arrest:

To be found in possession of a book issued by the UN is regarded as a crime in our Trust Territory. For example, when Mr. Sipoufo Kemga Gaspard was arrested in a train at 4:40 PM on 5 Aug 1956 by Gerard Prestat, Chief Subdivision Officer of Mbanga,

---

[13] Ibid.
[14] Ibid.

the latter snatched from him a book entitled UDHR and burned it.[15]

In the midst of this fracas, the Trusteeship Council made a decision regarding the processing of petitions from the Trusteeship territories, due to the dramatic increase from the Cameroons. During their 20th session, the council adopted a resolution to classify all petitions into one of five categories and summarize their contents into one document before discussing them. Only "specific petitions" would be addressed individually. [16] Nevertheless, we can still piece together an idea, and certainly a visual image of the process of petitioning. For example, from 16 February to 3 March 1959, the Trusteeship Council processed 513 petitions of which 357 were addressed to the Visiting Mission, and were dated from November and December 1958:

> *They were received by the Secretary-General towards the end of February 1959 in large envelopes, each containing thirty to forty petitions, posted in the Cameroons under British administration or Tunisia. Most of these petitions consist of a few words scribbled on a scrap of paper, demanding the unification and independence of the two Territories, with an initial or fingerprint instead of a signature. Twenty of these petitions addressed to the Visiting Mission contain a fuller statement.*[17]

---

[15] Petition from Mrs. Genevieve Magapgo, housewife, Babété, Mbouda, Bamileke Region, c/o Central Council of UDEFEC, Kumba, Kamerun under British administration, 3 Dec 1956, T/PET.5/L.320.

[16] ORTC, 20th Session, Annexes, Agenda Item 9, T/L.777, Resolution 1713, 20 May- 12 July 1957, Supplement 1.

[17] 513 petitions raising general problems concerning the Cameroons under British administration and the Cameroons under French administration, March 1959, T/PET.4&5/L.43.

The fuller statements included demands for immediate and unconditional amnesty for political prisoners, exiles, and members of the progressive movements; "the right to freely exercise democratic freedom;" "the restoration of calm and a normal political atmosphere;" the "withdrawal of French and British troops;" and "a referendum on the unification of the two territories."[18]

It is not difficult to picture the remaining UPC, JDC, and UDEFEC "leaders," traveling around, encouraging people to prepare petitions for the arrival of the 1958 Visiting Mission. As paper had become a precious commodity, following the ransacking of their supplies, the scribes would have had to tear off pieces, and scribble out the requisite demands, quickly, to allow more people the opportunity to put their fingerprint on the scrap of paper sent off to work its magic in New York.

The UPC, UDEFEC, and the JDC, officially banned in both territories, its leaders in exile or in hiding in the *maquis*, began to unravel. The act of popular petitioning remained, however, and the increasing number of petitions demonstrated that the movement's popularity had outgrown dependence on its leaders. The act of petitioning kept the movement afloat, by encouraging it to keep a unified front, by reminding members that the movement was larger than their own small locale. Without the traveling leadership delegations, the distribution of up-to-date information was limited, and members did not have the same awareness of pertinent issues beyond their own homes. Nevertheless, petitioners remained conscious of the overall goals of the nationalist struggle. The awareness of the UN was constant, as was a knowledge of the administrations' suppression of the

---

[18] Ibid.

UPC, the forced deportation of its leaders, and the fervent hope that those leaders would be returned to usher in the independence and reunification that remained the objective of the movement. In early 1959, Poline Matachange, a farmer from Bamendje wrote:

> *We women of Kamerun want to have back our husbands who have been imprisoned and those who have fled to the bush and thirteen children from Kamerun. The British Government arrested them and sent them far away from this country. We want them to return to their homes.*[19]

The act of petitioning had enabled the movement to take on a life of its own and provided it with foundations that even the violent repression of the movement could not shatter.

In the final years of the Trusteeship, there surfaces a disjointed body of petitions from a people without hope. Gone is the evidence of the seamless, unifying strategy distributed by UPC and UDEFEC leaders. Nevertheless, the legacy of that ideology remained. All the petitions on file originating from members of UPC, UDEFEC, JDC, or UNIKAMERUN contained the requisite demands for unification and independence.[20] Throughout 1959, the UN

---

[19] Petition from Poline Matachange, Farmer, Central Quarter, Bamendje, 10 Dec 1958, T/PET.5/1399.

[20] Towards the end of the trusteeship period, petitioners such as Mrs. Rachel Ndambouen had begun to suspect the UN's complicity in facilitating the repression of the nationalist movements in the Cameroons: "Since there are many colonialist hirelings in the Trusteeship Council plotting to put an end to the Kamerunians before the unification and independence of Kamerun I should like my petition to be submitted to the United Nations General Assembly. ... If indeed the UN accepts the *loi-cadre* Minister whom the French Government has set up at Yaoundé in

received petitions from Cameroonians throughout the territory, denouncing Ahidjo as Prime Minister and referring to his administration as the "puppet government" in Yaoundé. They requested the return of the exiled UPC leaders, and a round table discussion to decide Cameroon's political future. Meanwhile, more and more petitions advocating for the nationalists came from outside the territory.[21] Despite the administrations' military repression of the Bamileke and Bassa regions, the nationalist movement was not suppressed. As Cameroon approached independence, it was a nation made up, in large part, of political outsiders, and many of whom were geographically, as well as politically, outside the nation.

The petitions tell the history of a popular nationalist movement that took root among the population until it no longer depended on leadership for its survival. But how does a historian account for so popular a politics? How does one explain a movement that took root so firmly in the minds and lives of so many men, women, and youth throughout

---

their puppet assembly we can inform you that this year, 1959, we are prepared and we condemn your resolution on the question of Kamerun in 1959." Petition from Mrs. Rachel Ndambouen concerning the Cameroons under British administration and the Cameroons under French administration, T/PET.4&5/47.

[21] For example, from the Kamerun National Union in Ghana, from the UPC Information Office in Rabat, Morocco, and from members, particularly young Cameroonians abroad, who joined the World Federation of Democratic Youth, and wrote from Hungary, Czechoslovakia, Romania and Germany. In 1959, the UN received hundreds of individual postcards from members of WFDY from all over the world. See T/PET.4&5/L.39 and Add. 1, Add. 2, Add. 3. What was more, nationalists outside the territory remained the most vehement activists. Many of them were educated, and underwent military training during their years of exile. Interviews with Ngapeth-Biyong, Feze and Ekwe.

133

Cameroon that they continued to risk everything simply to keep writing about it, as though the sheer number of their pleas would bring about the liberation they imagined? In order to understand the history of UPC nationalism through its rank-and-file members rather than through its leaders, we must approach it through the Cameroonian women nationalists of UDEFEC and through the writings that supported and shaped the popular nationalism - the petitions to the UN.

Cameroonian Women and the Creation of a Popular Politics

Cameroonian women nationalists helped to shape the political imaginary of the Cameroonian population, enabling the evolution of an ideology that rejected colonialism and created a separate ideological terrain for popular discourse and interaction. Petitioning women believed there to be five thousand French troops in the Sanaga-Maritime; they informed members that the administration planned to exterminate nationalists by threatening biological fertility and the mental health of schoolchildren. They cited death, imprisonment, forced exile, destruction of property, and bullet-riddled corpses found in waterways as further evidence of the colonialists' extermination project. They described the "immediate appetites" of the colonialists for the "bananas, coffee, cocoa, and oil of the Cameroons," and accused the administration of "wanting to rule the Trust Territory as if it were a colony." [22] Women of UDEFEC depicted the

---

[22] 78 Petitions Raising General Problems concerning the Cameroons under French Administration, 13 June 1958, T/PET.5/L.455. Although

134

European administrations as a "ravening lion,"[23] that sought to kill Cameroonians and "eat" their wealth. These women nationalists helped launch a popular effort to claim independence in the collective imaginary - in the invisible world that explained and restructured the visible. [24] This represented a shift in "political thinkability" [25] for the Cameroonian population that adhered to UPC ideology - gradually undermining the "political thinkability" of foreign administration until it became unsustainable in the minds of the people.

The women of UDEFEC - who wrote petitions, expressing their own concerns and those of the nationalist movement of which they were a part and linking them to principles contained in the UN Charter - take their place in the slim ranks of African women nationalists who figure in the scholarship. The history of the women of UDEFEC offers a new perspective on African women's role in nationalist politics, however. The women of UDEFEC, whether educated urban-dwellers or illiterate rural farmers, literally wrote themselves into the nationalist movement. [26] By

---

this group of petitions is not sorted according to individual senders, this paragraph is attributed to a "group of women."

[23] Petition from Aguemani Elisabeth, Bafia, 30 Aug 1956, T/PET.5/949.

[24] See chap. 5.

[25] For Schatzberg, all societies - varying in time and place - have a moral matrix defining the politically "thinkable" vs. the "unthinkable" and societies will behave within this matrix until pushed to change by crisis, internal political movements which tap into the same moral matrix, or due to outside influences. Schatzberg, *Political Legitimacy*, chap. 1.

[26] Here, the women of UDEFEC differ fromthe women of the Usambara Citizens Union in Tanganyika who "appear in the archival materials of the period as an undifferentiated mass." Women in Feierman's analysis were unnamed: their political resistance went unnoticed because, illiterate, they did not write petitions to the UN, and according to Feierman, their "political resistance did not usually lead to arrest, because women were

way of UDEFEC's traveling leaders, from local committee to regional committee, and through the informal messages passed along by JDC couriers responsible for posting petitions, Cameroonian women got to hear the stories of other women with whom they shared similar concerns and fears. UDEFEC created an outlet for these women's complaints, both among their peers throughout the territory and within the international sphere of the UN. For the political leaders of UDEFEC, the women's stories provided fodder for the cause for independence and reunification. For the women planters and villagers who attended the meetings, volunteered their stories, and turned them into petitions, UDEFEC offered a place to come together and be heard. Whether or not the petitioning women became "nationalists" in the process, the growing awareness – facilitated by UDEFEC – of other women in similar situations began to link them together across regions, from rural to urban spaces, allowing them to identify with other women in a common cause.

Studying the position of African women through their role as nationalists adds a layer to the history of African women. Far more common are histories of African women agriculturalists, which made significant contributions to our understandings of the economic role of women in society.[27]

---

usually seen as having no public standing." Steven Feierman, *Peasant Intellectuals: Anthropology and History in Tanzania,* Madison, 1990, 219.

[27] Many of these studies originated in neo-Marxist materialist scholarship, analyzed women's contributions to the political economy of the colonial and postcolonial state. For example, Elizabeth Eldredge, "Women in Production: The Economic Role of Women in 19th Century Lesotho," *Signs: Journal of Women in Culture and Society,* 16.4 (1991); and Miriam Goheen, *Men Own the Fields, Women Own die Crops: Gender and Power in the Cameroon Grassfields,* Madison, 1996. For an approach that is more cultural than economic, see Henrietta Moore and Megan Vaughan, *Cutting Down*

More recently, African women have figured prominently in histories of medicine in Africa, allowing researchers to evaluate, in particular, women's bodies and biological fertility. [28] Another important portion of the history of African women has been devoted to their roles in the spiritual realm.[29]

Evaluating the role of women in African nationalism necessitates a combination of all of these approaches in order to understand how a social crisis posed by political conflict enabled women activists to effect change in the realms of agriculture, biological fertility, spirituality and medicine, as well as politics, all at once. Certainly some women seeking to ameliorate their position within Cameroonian society saw an opportunity to do so in the formation of UDEFEC. Others were prompted by the progressive ideals of a nationalism guided by the Universal Declaration of Human Rights to make claims for women's economic freedom, women's education, improved health care systems, and a general improvement in the status of women in Cameroonian society. As women participated in the nationalist movement in Cameroon, they helped to construct and popularize a nationalist movement, and at the same time that movement

---

Trees: Gender, Nutrition and Agricultural change in the Northern Province of Zambia, 1890-1990, Portsmouth, NH, London, and Lusaka, 1994.

[28] Nancy Rose Hunt, *A Colonial Lexicon: Of Birth Ritual, Medicalization and Mobility in the Congo*, Durham and London, 1999, Pamela Feldman-Savelsberg, *Plundered Kitchens, Empty Wombs: Threatened Reproduction and Identity in the Cameroon Grassfields*, Ann Arbor, 1999, and Lynn Thomas, *Politics of the Womb: Reproduction and the State in Kenya*, Berkeley and Los Angeles, 2003.

[29] Cynthia Hoehler-Fatton, *Women of Fire and Spirits: History, Faith, and Gender in Roho Religion in Western Kenya*, Oxford, 1996; Dorothy Hodgson, *The Church of Women: Gendered Encounters Between Maasai and Missionaries*, Bloomington, 2005.

informed their identities as Cameroonian women, redefining their role as women within society.[30] But it is important to emphasize that UDEFEC was not an explicitly feminist movement and leaders did not define it as such. Rather, the women of UDEFEC viewed their party as complimenting and in many ways extending the nationalist movement into the social realm of economic autonomy for agriculturalists and market women, education for children, maternity and infant care, and so on. In many ways UDEFEC's history lends itself to a "womanist" rather than "feminist" analysis. UDEFEC's mobilization unfolded within the context of a territory-wide struggle for national liberation and men were "a part of the change that [they] envisage[d]."[31]

Focusing on women's role in spreading information about the party and reshaping the peoples' ideology provides a new and effective way of understanding the UPC's popularity. UPC nationalism achieved popular success because of its compatibility with the established patterns of gender relations in many of the regions throughout the territory. Men and women worked together towards a common goal, but organized separately. It was the UPC's decentralization of its leadership, both through its reliance on local committees and its delegation of women that ensured its

---

[30] The critique of a centralized, uniform gender analysis imposed on diverse societies is one of the most prominent among African scholars writing about gender. See, for example, Oyeronke Oyewumi, *The Invention of Women: Making an African Sense of Western Gender Discourses,* Minneapolis, 1997, 1-30 and Ifi Amadiume, *Reinventing Africa: Matriarchy, Religion, and Culture,* London and New York, 1997, 161-82. On the construction of gender, see Sherry B. Ortner, *Making Gender: The Politics and Erotics of Culture,* Boston, 1996, 1-42.

[31] Susan Arndt, "African Gender Trouble and African Womanism: An Interview with Chikwenye Ogunyemi and Wanjiri Muthoni," *Signs* 25.3 (2000): 709-26.

rapid growth. UPC nationalism differed in this respect from the later "top down" politics of President Ahidjo who quickly excluded women from politics.[32]

The decentralization of UPC leadership combined with Um Nyobé's conscious efforts allowed Cameroonian nationalism to flourish beyond the political divisions attributed to ethnicism, commonly cited as characteristic of postcolonial African politics.

UPC and UDEFEC leaders reminded members to fight against "tribalism" and both directors' committees were ethnically diverse. The French administration's strategy of uprooting UPC leaders from Yaoundé or Douala and resettling them in remote areas facilitated the spread of the party, and encouraged nationalists, early on, to have faith in leaders who were not from their own area. The forced relocation of political activists on a large scale, beginning with the French ban of the party in 1955 and the migration of nationalists to the British territory, minimized ethnic divides in favor of anti-colonial solidarity, and lessened the symbolic importance of the Anglo-French boundary. The travels galvanized by the British and French administrations' repression caused people to mix with each other in ways that they had not before. Migration had been common in Cameroon throughout the colonial period and before, as people sought or were recruited for labor, settled on new lands, or were drawn by opportunities in trade. The displacement of nationalists, however, occurred along new geographical routes, and migrants carried with them a new, politicized consciousness of the reasons for their travels.

---

[32] Chantal Ndami, "La dynamique de la participation des femmes a la vie politique: le cas du Parlement camerounais, 1960-1997," MA Thesis, Université de Yaoundé-I, 1997, 37-40.

Often, they found themselves in situations where they relied upon each other and their host communities for survival.

The process of women nationalists in helping to mold the minds and imaginations of the people offer a new look at African nationalism, at least as it unfolded in Cameroon. This was a nationalism that had little to do with the formation of complex strategies and policies, although UPC and UDEFEC leadership were concerned with those essential details. Rather, this was a nationalism that had everything to do with a popular participation that, once it reached a certain point, provided its own momentum. That party members from throughout the territory and beyond continued to petition the UN, even after the disintegration of their leadership, and even after Um Nyobé's assassination – an event at first unknown to most of the petitioners – demonstrates that their motivation did not come from a handful of leaders. Instead, they were pushed forward by one another, guided by their belief in the UN as their ultimate savior. The idea of universal justice declared by the UN combined with the understanding of foreign administrators as dangerous to the social well-being. That combination made the goal of independence and reunification as the means to achieve justice and eradicate foreign dominance an easy pill to swallow. The magic formula was infinitely malleable - it could be individualized to speak for one petitioner or collectivized to speak for ten thousand of them.[33]

---

[33] In March 1958, the UN received 266 mimeographed copies of a petition bearing, in total, 10,640 signatures, and 190 copies of a petition bearing, in total, 8,355 signatures. The dates on the petitions varied from 2 Jan to 15 Feb 1958. Both petitions were sent from Bamenda. 456 petitions concerning general problems in the Cameroons under British administration and the Cameroons under French administration, T/PET.4 and 5/L.23.

The Nationalism of Petitions to the UN

The petitions provide a means of measuring the popularity of a nationalist movement that outlived its leadership. Within the petitionary records, we see the outlines of a popular politics taking shape. The two strains of narrative - one originating from the Western-educated leaders of UDEFEC, and the other coming from mostly illiterate village women or city laborers - represented the two-fold strategy conceived by Um Nyobé at the UPC's inception. On the one hand, urban members appealed to Western human rights advocates using an international political rhetoric. On the other, members throughout the territories expressed their rejection of the European administrations in their own words, focusing on their lands, their crops, their health and the health of their communities and families, and the education of their children. [34] The two languages began to blend as women led the way in appropriating the principles of the UN, especially those expressed in the Universal Declaration of Human Rights. Cameroonian women claimed their right to free education for children, adequate health care for themselves and their children, economic equality between the

---

[34] Marthe Moumié wrote in *Femmes camerounaises* in June 1955 that "the Cameroonian people is [sic] asking for its independence, not as a favor, but as a right which it is justified in demanding in accordance with Articles 2, 3, 4, 5, 6, and 7 of the Universal Declaration of Human Rights." Petition from the editorial board of the newspaper *Femmes camerounaises* concerning the Cameroons under French administration, 7 June 1955 T/PET.5/618. Mme Ngapeth-Biyong explained that the Universal Declaration of Human Rights supported them in their efforts, and they attempted to distribute as many copies as possible. Interview with Ngapeth-Biyong. In 1956, the General Assembly of UDEFEC committees requested the General Assembly "to send us a copy of the Universal Declaration of Human Rights." UDEFEC, Central Committees of the Bamileke Region, General Assembly, 10 Nov 1956, T/PET.5/984.

sexes, and decried the administration's repression of the nationalists that left women without their husbands, or subjected them to gendered torture, such as rape or genital electrocution.

Recognizing the importance of a notion of universal human rights and UN principles, petitioning women often requested more information, as though this, in itself, would liberate them. Rebecca Ngo Nyoth, a dressmaker from Bipundi, in the Sanaga-Maritime, requested:

> *the transmission of the records of all the debates on the Kamerunian question in the Trusteeship Council and the Standing Committee on Petitions from 1952 onwards, the reports of the Trusteeship Council for 1955, and the report of the famous Dorsinville Visiting Mission, so that I may be informed about the Kamerunian question.*[35]

In July 1959, after the UN had dissolved its trusteeship over the Cameroons, Marguerite Madefo requested copies of

> *the UN Charter, the Trusteeship Agreement for East Kamerun, the Trusteeship Agreement for West Kamerun, the Universal Declaration of Human Rights, and the Rules of procedure of the General Assembly, to enable me to know better my country's international position.*[36]

---

[35] Petition from Rebecca Ngo Nyoth, *Maquis*, 13 July 1956, T/PET.5/919.

[36] Petition from Mrs. Marguerite Madefo concerning the Cameroons under British and French administrations, Bafang, 9 July 1959, T/PET.4&5/46. Mrs. Madefo's request came after the UN had dissolved its Trusteeship over the Cameroons (March 1959).

The popularity of the Universal Declaration of Human Rights and the UN Charter indicates that the nationalists recognized the compatibility of their pro-independence ideology, and the international trend toward human rights. Supported by the UN - an international body perceived as an ideological advocate for the rights of the Cameroonian people - Cameroonian women untiringly and incessantly appealed to the UN to fulfill the role they attributed to it. The act of petitioning reinforced the concept of the UN as liberating savior, which in turn contributed to the popularity of the nationalist movement. The UN provided a constant reminder that the demands for liberation from foreign administration were validated in a wider international sphere.

The appropriation of UN ideology and human rights narratives in the local political discourses of Cameroonian nationalists elucidates the creation of a grassroots political "imaginary." Local participation in the political process did not depend only upon the translation of nationalistic concepts into local languages[37] or on the symbolic revival of "traditional" rituals to serve as interpretative metaphors[38] for the political crisis sparked by UPC nationalism, but also on the inhabitants' conceptions of UN principles and language. The creation of the imaginary drew upon "traditional" symbols and rites that pre-dated colonialism, but also upon new ingredients introduced by the UN. Likewise, the leaders

---

[37] See Mbembe, *Naissance*, chap. 9 for an analysis of the role of translation in shaping the political imaginary of the people.

[38] Ibid., 361, 362. The "rehabilitation" of rites such as the *ngee* (which included the fabrication of poisons from human bones), or *ngambi* (divination), reactivated the "imaginary" that underwrote them. See also Florence Bernault, *Démocraties ambigües en Afrique centrale: Congo-Brazzaville, Gabon: 1940-65*, Paris, 1996, especially 328-338 for a discussion of the construction of political power out of "traditional" cultural references combined with the new and "modern" ideas inherited from colonialism.

of the UPC and UDEFEC did not feel compelled to edit the language of petitioners from rural areas, as did Shambaa "peasant intellectuals" writing against the chiefship. The crucial issue in Shambaa local politics - rainmaking - was excluded from petitions to the UN because petitioners "would all have known that it was inappropriate and counterproductive to write to London or New York about healing the land." [39] In the case of the Cameroonian nationalist movement, however, the Cameroonian petitions demonstrate an exchange as UPC and UDEFEC leadership distributed UN principles and petitioners wrote back with local understandings of what those principles meant to them.

From their first, tentative steps towards involvement in the UPC movement, the Cameroonian women of UDEFEC had become militant political activists within less than a decade. By the time of the UN's lifting of the trusteeship from Cameroon on 14 March 1959, Cameroonian women nationalists had helped the movement outgrow its dependence on its leadership. The political imaginary brought into being by the women and men who believed in the UPC nationalist movement had no place in President Ahmadou Ahidjo's new order. Not dead, yet prohibited from living, present only in hiding, this political imaginary rested uneasily in the social memory of the Cameroonian population, and contributes still to the dysfunctionality of the postcolonial state.[40]

[39] Feierman, *Peasant Intellectuals*, 210.
[40] Mbembe, "Pouvoir," 223-29 and A. Mbembe. "Provisional Notes from the Postcolony," *Africa* 62.1 (1992): 3-37.

Bibliography

Archival Sources

Archives Nationales de Yaounde, UDEFEC files
United Nations Micro-Print Series, 1946-1960: E/CN.6
    T/C.2/L T/C.2/SR T/COM.4/L T/OBS.4 T/PET.4
    T/PET.4/L T/PET.4 & 5 T/PET.5

Interviews

Ekwe, Henriette. Douala, 18 June 1999.
Feze, Marcel Ngandjong. Bandenkop, 15 July 1999.
Loucka, Basile. Yaoundé, 3 July 1999.
Mbarga, Gérard. Yaoundé, 19 July 1999.
Ngapeth-Biyong, Marie-Irene. Yaounde, 6 July 1999.
Ngayo Teclaire, Nicaise. Bangangte, 16 July 1999.
Njike-Bergeret, Claude. Bangangte, 15 July 1999.
Tchatchouang Waton Paul. Bangwa, 16 July 1999.

Contemporary Sources:

Amadiume, Ifi. *Reinventing Africa: Matriarchy, Religion, and Culture.*
London and New York, 1997.

Ardener, Shirley, "Sexual Insult and Female Militancy," in Shirley
Ardener, ed. *Perceiving Women.* London, 1975.

Arndt, Susan. "African Gender Trouble and African Womanism: An Interview with Chikwenye Ogunyemi and Wanjiri Muthoni." *Signs* 25.3 (2000): 709-26.

Barbier, Jean-Claude. *Femmes du Cameroun: Mères pacifiques, femmes rebelles.* Paris, 1985.

Bayart, Jean-François, et al. *Le politique par le bas en Afrique noire: Contributions à une problématique de la démocratie.* Paris, 1992.

--------------------. "Le politique par le bas en Afrique noire," *Politique Africaine* 1.1 (1981): 53-82.

--------------------. *L'Etat au Cameroun.* 1979, Paris, 2nd ed., 1985.

Bernault, Florence. *Démocraties ambigües en Afrique centrale. Congo-Brazzaville, Gabon: 1940-1965.* Paris, 1996.

Biya, Ndebi. *Etre, pouvoir et génération: Le système mbok chez les Basa du Sud-Cameroun.* Paris, 1987.

Bjornson, Richard. *The African Quest for Freedom and Identity: Cameroonian Writing and National Experience.* Bloomington, 1991.

Bogin, Ruth. "Petitioning and the New Moral Economy of Post-Revolutionary America." *The William and Mary Quarterly* 45.3 (1998): 391-425.

Chilver, E. M. "Women Cultivators, Cows and Cash Crops: Phyllis Kayberry's Women of the Grassfields Revisited." In P. Geschiere and P. Konings, eds. Conference on the Political Economy of Cameroon - Historical Perspectives. African Studies Center Research Report 35. Leiden, 1989: 383-421.

Connelly, Matthew. *A Diplomatic Revolution: Algeria's Fight for Independence and the Origins of the Post–Cold War Era.* Oxford: Oxford University Press, 2002.

Coquery-Vidrovitch, Catherine. *Les Africaines: Histoire des femmes d'Afrique noire du XIXè an XXè siècle.* Paris, 1994.

Criaud, Jean. *Le geste des Spiritains: Histoire de l'Eglise au Cameroun, 1916-1990.* Yaoundé, 1990.

Débarge, J. *La Mission médicale au Cameroun.* Paris, 1934.

Deltombe, Thomas, Manuel Domergue and Jacob Tatsitsa. *Kamerun: Une guerre cachée aux origines de la Françafrique (1948–1971).* Paris: La Découverte, 2011.

De Rosny, Eric. *L'Afrique des guérisons,* Paris, 1992.

Desan, Suzanne. "Reconstituting the Social after the Terror: Family, Property and the Law in Popular Politics." *Past and Present: A Journal of Historical Studies* 164 (1999): 81-121.

den Ouden, J. H. B. "Incorporation and Changes in the Composite Household. The Effects of Coffee

Introduction and Food Crop Commercialization in Two Bamileke Chiefdoms, Cameroon." In C. Presvelou and S. Spijkers-Zwart, eds. *The Household, Women and Agricultural Development.* Wageningen, 1980.

Deschamps, Hubert. "French Colonial Policy in Tropical Africa between the Two World Wars." In Prosser Gifford and William Roger Louis, eds., *France and Britain in Africa: Imperial Rivalry and Colonial Rule.* New Haven and London, 1971: 543-569.

Diduk, Susan. "Women's Agricultural Production and Political Action in the Cameroon Grassfields." *Africa* 59 (1989): 338-55.

Dongmo, Jean-Louis. *Le dynamisme bamileke.* Vol. I: *La maîtrise de l'espace agraire.* Yaoundé, 1981.

Eldredge, Elizabeth. "Women in Production: The Economic Role of Women in 19th Century Lesotho." *Signs: Journal of Women in Culture and Society* 16.4 (1991).

Eteki-Otabela, Marie-Louise. "Dix ans de luttes du collectif des femmes pour le renouveau: quelques reflexions pour le mouvement féministe camerounais." *Recherches féministes,* 5.1 (1992): 125-34.

------------------------. *Misère et grandeur de la démocratie au Cameroun.* Paris, 1987.

Feierman, Steven. *Peasant Intellectuals: Anthropology and History in Tanzania.* Madison, 1990.

Feldman-Savelsberg, Pamela. *Plundered Kitchens, Empty Wombs: Threatened Reproduction and Identity in the Cameroon Grassfields.* Ann Arbor, 1999.

Gardinier, David E. *Cameroon: United Nations Challenge to French Policy.* London, 1963.

Geiger, Susan. *TANU Women: Gender and Culture in the Making of Tanganyikan Nationalism, 1955-1965.* Portsmouth, 1997. 62

-----------. "Women and African Nationalism." Journal of Women's History 2.1 (1990): 227-244.

-----------. "Women in Nationalist Struggle: TANU Activists in Dar Es Salaam." *International Journal of African Historical Studies* 20: 1 (1987): 1-26.

Geschiere, Peter. *The Modernity of Witchcraft: Politics and the Occult in Postcolonial Africa.* Charlottesville, 1997.

----------------. "Hegemonic Regimes and Popular Protest: Bayart, Gramsci and the State in Cameroon." In Wim M. J. van Binsbergen, Filip Reyntjens, and Gerti Hesseling, eds. *State and Local Community in Africa.* Brussels, 1986.

Glissant, Edouard. Poetics of Relation. Trans. Betsy Wing. Ann Arbor, 1997.

Goheen, Miriam. *Men Own the Fields, Women Own the Crops: Gender and Power in the Cameroon Grassfields.* Madison, 1996.

Guyer, Jane. "The Food Economy and French Colonial Rule in Central Cameroun." *Journal of African History* 19 (1978): 577-597.

Hess, Robert L. *Italian Colonialism in Somalia.* Chicago, 1966.

Hodgson, Dorothy. *The Church of Women: Gendered Encounters Between Maasai and Missionaries,* Bloomington: Indiana University Press, 2005.

Hoehler-Fatton, Cynthia. *Women of Fire and Spirit: History, Faith and Gender in Roho Religion in Western Kenya.* Oxford, 1996.

Hunt, Nancy Rose. *A Colonial Lexicon: Of Birth Ritual, Medicalization and Mobility in the Congo.* Durham, 1999.

Hunt, Nancy Rose, Tessie P. Liu and Jean Quataert, eds. *Gendered Colonialisms in African History.* Oxford and Maiden, MA, 1997.

Johnson-Odim, Cheryl. "On Behalf of Women and the Nation: Funmilayo Ransome-Kuti and the Struggles for Nigerian Independence and Women's Equality." In Cheryl Johnson-Odim and Margaret Strobel, eds. *Expanding the Boundaries of Women's History: Essays on Women in the Third World.* Bloomington, 1992. 144-157.

Johnson-Odim, Cheryl and Nina Emma Mba. *For Women and the Nation: Funmilayo Ransome-Kuti of Nigeria.* Chicago, 1997.

Joseph, Richard. *Radical Nationalism in Cameroun: The Social Origins of the UPC Rebellion.* Oxford, 1977.

--------------. "Nationalism in Postwar Cameroon: The Difficult Birth of the UPC." *Journal of African Studies* 2.2 (1975): 201 -29.

--------------. "Settlers, Strikers and Sans-Travail: The Douala Riots of September 1945." *Journal of African History* 25.4 (1975): 65-90.

Ilumoka, Adetoun O. "African Women's Economic. Social, and Cultural Rights - Toward a Relevant Theory and Practice." In Rebecca Cook, ed. *Human Rights of Women: National and International Perspectives.* Philidelphia, 1995.

Kofele-Kale, Ndiva. "Ethnicity, Regionalism, and Political Power: A Post-Mortem of Ahidjo." In Michael Schatzberg and I. William Zartman, eds. *The Political Economy of Cameroon.* New York, 1986.

Konings, Piet. *Gender and Class in the Tea Estates of Cameroon.* Leiden, 1995.

Le Vine, Victor. "Leadership and Regime Changes in Perspective." In Michael Schatzberg and I. William Zartman, eds. *The Political Economy of Cameroon.* New York, 1986: 20-52.

Levy, M. F. *Each in Her Own Way: Five Women Leaders of the Developing World.* Boulder, 1988.

Mark, Gregory A. "The Vestigial Constitution: The History and Significance of the Right to Petition." *Fordham Law Review* 66 (1998): 2153-2230.

Martin, Charles H. "Internationalizing 'The American Dilemma': The Civil Rights Congress and the 1951 Genocide Petition to the United Nations." *Journal of American Ethnic History* 16 (Summer 1997): 35-61.

Mba, Ninna Ema. *Nigerian Women Mobilized: Women's Political Activity in Southern Nigeria, 1900-1965*. Berkeley, 1982.

Mbapndah, Ndobegang M. "French Colonial Agricultural Policy, African Chiefs, and Coffee Growing in the Cameroun Grassfields, 1920-1960." *The International Journal of African Historical Studies* 27 (1994): 41-58.

Mbembe, Achille. *De la postcolonie: Essai sur L'imagination politique dans l'Afrique contemporaine*. Paris, 2000.

---------------. *La naissance du maquis dans le Sitd-Cameroun, 1920-1960*. Paris, 1996.

---------------. "Provisional Notes from the Postcolony." *Africa* 62.1 (1992): 3-37.

-----------------. "Pouvoir des morts et langage des vivants: Les errances de la mémoire nationaliste au Cameroun." In Jean-François Bayart, et al. eds., *Le politique par le bas: Contributions a une problématique de la démocratie*. Paris, 1992, 183-229.

----------------. "Domaines de la nuit et autorité onirique dans les maquis du sud-Cameroun (1955-1958)." *Journal of African History* 31 (1991): 89-121.

----------------. "Introduction". *Ecrits sous maquis*. By Ruben Um Nyobé. Paris, 1989, 1-42.

----------------. "Introduction". By Ruben Um Nyobé, *Le Problème National Kamerunais*. Paris, 1984.

Michel, Marc. "Une décolonisation confisquée? Perspectives sur la décolonisation du Cameroun sous tutelle de la France, 1955-1960." *Revue française d'histoire d'Outre-mer* 324-325 (1999): 229-258.

Moore, Henrietta and Megan Vaughan. *Cutting Down Trees: Gender, Nutrition and Agricultural Change in the Northern Province of Zambia, 1890-1990*. Portsmouth, NH, London, and Lusaka, 1994.

Mortimer, Edward. *France and the Africans 1944-1960: A Political History*. London, 1969.

Moumié, Marthe. *Victime du colonialisme français: Mon mari Félix Moumié*. Paris: Editions Duboiris, 2006.

Ndami, Chantal. "La dynamique de la participation des femmes à la vie politique: le cas du Parlement camerounais, 1960-1997." MA Thesis. University of Yaoundé I, 1997.

Ngapeth-Biyong, Marie-Irène. *Cameroun: Combats pour l'indépendance.* Paris: L'Harmattan, 2009.

Ngavirue, Zedekia. *Political Parties and Interest Groups in South West Africa (Namibia): A Study of a Plural Society.* Basel, 1997.

Njiké-Bergeret, Claude. *Ma passion africaine.* Paris, 1998.
Nkwi, Paul Nchoji and Jean-Pierre Warnier. *Elements for a History of the Western Grassfields.* Yaoundé, 1982.

Ongoum, Louis-Marie. "Erotic Poetry of the Grasslands." *Research in African Literatures* 24.2 (1993): 101-09.

Oyewumi, Oyeronke. *The Invention of Women: Making an African Sense of Western Gender Discourses.* Minneapolis and London, 1997.

Schatzberg, Michael. *Political Legitimacy in Middle Africa: Father, Family, Food.* Bloomington, 2001.

-----------------. "Power, Legitimacy and 'Democratisation' in Africa." *Africa* 63.4 (1993): 445-61.

Shanklin, Eugenia. "ANLU Remembered: The Kom Women's Rebellion of 1958-61." *Dialectical Anthropology* 15.2-3(1990): 159-82.

Spear, Thomas. *Mountain Farmers: Moral Economies of Land and Agricultural Development in Arusha and Meru.* Berkeley, 1997.

Spivak, Gayatri Chakravorty. *Outside in the Teaching Machine.* New York, 1993.

Staudt, Kathleen A. "Women's Politics, the State, and Capitalist Transformation in Africa." In Irving Leonard Markovitz, ed. *Studies in Power and Class in Africa.* Oxford, 1987.

Terretta, Meredith. "Cameroonian Nationalists Go Global: From Forest *Maquis* to a Pan-African Accra." *Journal of African History* 51.2 (2010): 189–212.

Terretta, Meredith. "Chiefs, Traitors and Representatives: The Construction of a Political Repertoire in Independence Era Cameroun." *International Journal of African Historical Studies* 43.2 (2010): 227-58.

Thomas, Lynn. *Politics of the Womb: Reproduction and the State in Kenya.* Berkeley and Los Angeles: University of California Press, 2003.

Titi Nwel, Pierre. *Thong Likeng, Fondateur de la religion de Nyambebantu.* Paris, 1986.

UDEFEC. *"Union Démocratique des Femmes Camerounaises.* Yaoundé, 1992?.

Um Nyobé, Ruben. *Ecrits sous maquis.* Achille Mbembe, ed. Paris. 1989.

Um Nyobé, Ruben. *Le problème national kamerunais.* Achille Mbembe, ed. Paris, 1984.

UDEFEC. *Union démocratique des femmes camerounaises.* Douala, 1992?.

Union des Populations du Kamerun. *L' u. p. c. parle...* Paris: François Maspero, 1971.

Union des Populations du Cameroun. *Les grandes lignes de la situation au Cameroun.* n.d. 196[?].

Union des Populations du Cameroun. "Memorandum submitted to the Conference of Independent African States Held at Addis Ababa, 14th-18th June, 1960." London: Union of the Populations of the Cameroons, [1960].

Union des Populations du Cameroun. *La Tutelle Internationale à l'épreuve.* Cairo: Le service de reformation de l'UPC a l'etranger, [1959?].

Union des Populations du Cameroun. *From Algeria to the Kamerun.* Cairo: Foreign Delegation of the Union of the Populations of the Cameroons, [1958?].

Union des Populations du Cameroun. *The UPC denounces the planned systematic tortures in the Kamerun.* Cairo: Bureau of Leading Committee of the Union of the Populations of the Cameroons, 1958.

Union des Populations du Cameroun. *The Kamerun.* Cairo, 1957.

Vansina, Jan. *Oral Tradition as History.* Madison, 1985.

Vaughan, Megan. *Curing their Ills: Colonial Power and African Illness*. Stanford, 1991.

Warnier, Jean-Pierre. *L'esprit d'entreprise au Cameroun*. Paris, 1993.

White, Luise. *Speaking with Vampires: Rumor and History in Colonial Africa*. Berkeley, 2000.

Women's International Democratic Federation. *Women's International Democratic Federation*, 1945-1965. Berlin, 1965.

--. "That they may Live; African Women Arise." Berlin, 1954.

--. "For their Rights as Mothers, Workers, Citizens." Berlin, 1952.

--. "The Rights of Women, Defence of Children, Peace." Berlin, n.d.

Wonyu, Eugene. *De l'UPC a l'UC: Témoignage à l'aube de l'Indépendance (1953-1961)*. Paris, 1985.

Wood, Betty. "White Women, Black Slaves, and the Law in Early National Georgia: The Sunbury Petition of 1791." *The Historical Journal* 35.3 (1992): 611-22.

Yana, Simon David. "Statuts et roles féminins au Cameroun: réalités d'hier, images d'aujourd'hui." *Politique Africaine* 65 (1997): 35-47.

CPSIA information can be obtained at www.ICGtesting.com
Printed in the USA
LVOW13s2353310114

371880LV00003B/68/P

9 789956 728053